OPUS 40

A Resource for Grading
Academic Writing

August 2010

With a CD of the MCT Comment Archive
for Grading Research Papers

Michael Clay Thompson

Royal Fireworks Press
Unionville, New York

Royal Fireworks Press
First Avenue, PO Box 399
Unionville, NY 10988-0399
(845) 726-4444
FAX: (845) 726-3824
email: mail@rfwp.com
website: rfwp.com

ISBN: 978-0-88092-697-3

Printed and bound in the United States of America using vegetable-
based inks on acid-free recycled paper and environmentally-friendly
cover coatings by the Royal Fireworks Printing Co. of Unionville, New York.

Design and text by Michael Clay Thompson

Table of Contents

91

Robert,

I thoroughly enjoyed your paper on Aristotle's ethics. You managed to
bring the ideas alive, and I think that you understood them accurately
and presented them clearly. Your paper has a clear essay structure and
a sharp thesis. You have also done a good job proofreading your paper;
I only found a few elementary errors (that is too many) to correct.
What the paper shows me is that you have the potential to develop into
a fine academic writer. If you continue to refine this talent, you will
be writing impressive papers in future courses. There are always some
problems that need correction, so let us look at a few of those. Some of
my comments will come from my computer archive of explanations.

You must adhere to the MLA format conventions. The principle reason that
I could not give the paper an A is that you deviated too often from the
MLA formatting conventions. Your margins are too wide, not one inch as
the standard requires. You have single-spaced your long quotes, when the
MLA standard requires you to double-space the entire paper. You have
commas in the headers at the top of the page, and you did not put the
periods in the correct places for your parentheticals. You also did not
alphabetize your Works Cited page. This is too many slips, and as we
discussed in class, MLA is worth one letter grade, so the most you could
receive for this paper was a B. It is a high B because the paper is so
outstanding otherwise.

Do not overuse hyphens.
Do not overuse hyphens at the ends of the lines. It is best to avoid
breaking words with hyphens, unless you break a very long word in its
middle. Otherwise, do not hyphenate in a way that leaves only one to
three letters of a word at the end of the line. It is better for the
right margin to be a bit more ragged than for the reader to find short
syllables of words at the ends of the lines. These short, incomplete
syllables are a slight interruption to the smooth flow of thought.

1. Introduction to the Annotated Comment Archive

This text with a research paper comment archive on CD has two potential purposes. One is to supplement my three-volume *Advanced Academic Writing* series, also published by Royal Fireworks Press, and the other is to offer a stand-alone resource for grading student papers.

Even the most successful teacher knows how it feels to work hard and come up short. As teachers, we often succeed, but we also sometimes form ambitious plans for student learning, only to find that for some reason—which we often cannot identify—our wonderful plan fails. We can be in denial about this outcome: the students do not care, the parents do not supervise at home, and other ways to avoid the ugly truth, but in the end we sit staring at the fact that does not die: our strategy did not work. We know, grimly, that if we use the same strategy again next year, it will fail again.

Some forty years ago, hence the title of th is book, I found myself in the gray clutch of such a gruesome fact: I was teaching high school and devoting serious classroom time to advanced academic writing—research papers, to be specific—and getting *nowhere*. We were going through all the standard motions, but we were the writing dead, stumbling and groaning from deadline to deadline, and all of us—me included—despised the entire process. When it finally ended, not with a bang but a whimper, all of us were glad. After mountains of work, the students still did not produce impressive academic papers; they still did not feel that they knew what to do; they still did not see the point, and they hoped they would not have to write another. This was not what I had hoped for, at all.

I was more frustrated than the students were. I cared. I knew it was important. I had tried everything, and I did not know what was wrong. I had tried numerical point systems, busy rubrics, and trendy student-centered writing projects. I had gone to workshops; I had assigned journals; I had stood on my head. I had tried to let students pick their own topics without restriction. I had tried breaking the paper assignments down into a long series of simpler deadlines, a deadline for each component of the process (thesis, note cards, bibliography cards, outline, rough draft, second rough draft, final paper, revision of final paper, *ad nauseam*). I had lectured and threatened and stomped and steamed. No soap. Oddly, every other part of the course went well, and we all liked one another; chemistry was not the problem.

The problem was my process. I needed a different strategy. I needed a strategy strong enough to change my students, who were nowhere near ready to write academic research papers, into academic writers. I needed a strategy that made writers, not one that had us going through the wasted motions of fleeting units and flurried activities.

The Students

My students were not the cause of the problem. The students I was teaching had much in common with millions of other students. They did not have the foundation that they needed for academic writing. As a group they had characteristics many teachers will recognize. They had studied grammar in previous years, but the study had been partial and sporadic, not imparting the comprehensive four-level command (parts of speech, parts of sentence, phrases, and clauses) that enables students to avoid bad grammar or to punctuate grammar correctly. They had studied grammar but had not learned it. They had done stacks of writing, but the bulk of the writing they had done was in informal genres such as journals, opinion responses, and short stories, leaving them clueless about the expectations, standards, and style of academic writing. Repeatedly, their writing practices (gag me with a *prompt*) had been of the personal response type, on hollow topics that anyone can write about, in first person, without knowledge. They had written often but had not written standard English—what we once thought of as *normal school writing*. They had also studied vocabulary, but the words they had studied had been random and idiosyncratic, had been presented as self-contained vocabulary worksheets, and had not been reinforced by strong literature containing those words because their primary reading experience had been textbooks from which such words are methodically removed by sales-minded publishers. The age-graded vocabulary program had been dumbed-down—gutted—with hundreds of basic words necessary to the appreciation of even children's classics (*Peter Pan*, *The Wind in the Willows*) deferred to higher grade levels. Students had studied word lists but had read wordless textbooks. Their literature had consisted of short, dumbed-down excerpts in literature anthologies, supplemented by a few low-vocabulary classics such as *The Old Man and The Sea*. They had never read strong, long, non-textbook nonfiction, which was the genre I asked them to write in their research papers. They had visited the school library but had never mastered the library or learned how to read or take notes from academic sources. In short the students were not ready to write academic papers, nor were they close; the students had neither written nor even read the kind of language I wanted in my annual research paper assignment. They simply did not know what it was, did not know what it sounded like, did not know what I wanted, had no experience of it. Their entire reading lives had been only schooly, never scholarly. Not until I became realistic about the unacademic school-lives of the students would I perceive the nature of a writing program that would transform them.

Without belaboring the trial-and-error saga that led to a solution, let me just say that after years of teaching academic writing in middle school and high school English and history courses (I taught both, at different times), I finally arrived at a method that works. It is not effortless, but it is a winner. It makes an academic writer of every student in the class. If you as the teacher know academic grammar and punctuation rules, if you can type well, and if you have a computer that can open two word processing documents at one time, letting you copy from one document and paste to the other, you too can do this.

I should have known, but I did not, that the solution would be simple. Simpler than any of the failures. Simple enough to make the truth clear to the students. Simple enough to be right in front of my nose, all along. Simple enough to shed the pedantic for the authentic, to be something any real writer would recognize. Simple enough to be hard work without being busywork, either for me or for the students.

To solve the problem of teaching my students to write good academic papers, I had to change four things. First, I had to implement a thorough four-level grammar review in the first weeks of school, followed by a review of the grammar-based punctuation rules required in academic English. Any grammar strategy that did not present clauses until the spring was useless to me; the students would need the grammar to write good papers during the year. Second, I had to upgrade the quality and quantity of the literature they were reading, both fiction and nonfiction. Third, I had to give up the expectation that I could transform the students with only one major research paper, and fourth, I had to change the way I was grading.

I will not here elaborate the grammar strategy because that is the subject of my grammar texts, nor will I go into detail about the writing assignments and the content of the instruction because that is already available in the *Advanced Academic Writing* series.

My approach to literature has been described in *Classics in the Classroom*. What I will discuss here, briefly, is the multiple paper strategy and then, more elaborately, the grading method that is the purpose of this text.

The Strategy: One paper is not enough.

When my first efforts to teach academic writing did not succeed, I did the logical thing: I had allotted more time to the research paper, dividing it into more logical steps, and expanding the complexity. The more I broke it down and increased the time I was spending on details, the worse things got. Trying to get the students to see the forest, I was adding trees. After years of frustration, I realized what should have been obvious all along. Academic writing is too complicated to learn in one pass; students cannot do it once and get good, and it does not matter how much class time you throw at a one-paper plan. To master academic writing, students need to do the whole process, and then do the whole process again, and then do the whole process again, and again.

I had to change my model from a single massive paper with ten different deadlines to a college-style program of multiple short papers with single deadlines. The only deadline would be for the paper itself, just like college. In high school I had learned to do note cards, bibliography cards, outlines, rough drafts, final drafts, and revisions; in college no professor ever asked me for cards or outlines or rough drafts; they only wanted the paper, when it was due, and there were no rewrites. You had only one chance.

I also realized that students could learn from short papers. My experience showed that students made the same mistakes in a three-page paper that they made in a ten- or fifteen-page paper. I realized that just because I did not have deadlines for thesis and notes and outlines and rough drafts, that did not mean that I could not teach (some of) those things or help students during those phases. I would be supportive and available, but I would not expect those to be turned in or graded. I realized that some of the impedimenta of the orthodox method were no longer necessary or appropriate in an era of computer labs and laptops where word processors have outline processors built into the software.

I also thought about what the students would experience by having to do the entire process again and then again. For the second paper, it would no longer be their first time in the library, it would no longer be the first time they had read long academic nonfiction, it would no longer be the first time they had tried to find quotations or wrestle their information into an essay structure. It would be their second time, and then their third time, and their fourth time, and each time the strangeness would diminish. Each time the extraordinary would become ordinary, each time students would find more of the process obvious and would turn their attention to new aspects of the writing process.

As it turned out, four short papers, connected to the course content, in MLA format, did not absorb more class time than the one-paper method I had been using. I now had four deadlines instead of seven deadlines. Grading rough drafts then had taken longer than grading a second paper now. Grading revisions then took as long as grading a third paper now. Four weekends a year, I had to grade term papers. The effect on my course calendar was negligible, but the students were getting four full cycles instead of one.

The effect on achievement was dramatic. Finally, they had gone through the process enough times that they were no longer beginners. The first papers of the year were still rough—but this was as far as I had ever gotten before—and the papers in the second semester were wonderful. The papers were making students read, in many cases for the first time, large quantities of intellectual analysis and factual content—four times. They were slowly getting used to grown-up nonfiction, to grown-up intellectual life. Students were discovering what knowledge really is. Little by little, the papers were teaching students the reasons for rules of grammar and style, the importance of the rules, the fact that the rules were not just random or stupid or arbitrary. Students were beginning to see from personal experience that these research projects were giving them deep knowledge of topics that textbooks only skimmed. They were beginning to realize that they could be academically successful and that intellectual experience was not so bad after all. They were beginning to understand what it feels like to be proud of a paper they had written.

94

Maria,

Thank you for this strong paper on how Edwin Hubble's work with the Wilson telescope changed our concept of the universe. I enjoyed reading your paper, and this was because you not only selected an exciting intellectual thesis, but you also wrote the paper to such a high academic standard that I rarely had to stop reading, either because your writing was unclear or to correct errors. Your English is excellent, your MLA format is almost perfect, and your essay structure is crystal clear. This is so much better than your second paper--I am really impressed. I am particularly impressed with the outstanding quotations you found to support and illustrate your thesis; the quote by George Ellery Hale was perfect. There are always a few things to improve, so let us look at a few of those:

Unfounded assertions
There are certain kinds of assertions you should not make unless you can provide evidence for them, especially in a formal paper where you are not allowed to present something as a fact if it is not one. It is risky to make assertions about what most people think, or about what a famous person thought or intended. How do you know what most people think? How do you know what was in the private mind of another person? Unless you have some way to document such questionable assertions, avoid them.

Brackets [] within quotes
Use brackets [like this] for inserting words into quotations. When you insert words into quotations--usually for the purpose of clarifying references or enhancing the flow of the sentences--you must enclose your inserted words in brackets like [this] to show the reader that these words were not part of the original quote. Be sure to use [brackets] rather than (parentheses) or <mathematical symbols>.

Use a colon before subtitle
When you have a subtitle to the main title of your paper, use a colon between the title and subtitle. If both the title and subtitle are short

Grading affects writing.

The next element of writing instruction that I had to change was my grading method. Like a weary dieter, I had tried every touted trend: point systems, rubric-based grids like corporate spreadsheets, smiley praise systems that shirked calling a mistake a mistake—system after system that spoke fake language no real writer would recognize, flowcharts of steps no real writer would follow, scaffolds of strictness strange to a real writer's heart. I was assessing writing from a point of view outside of writing, from systems designed to meet teachers' needs. I was grading like a teacher, not like a writer.

My grading surgeries had been killing my patients. Most of these methods demoralized the students. Most of these methods were boring. Most of these methods ignored the very dramas that make writing exciting and powerful and personal and true. Most of these methods issued a suffocating cloud of pedagogical minutiae that blackened out the humanity of writing. I was trying to grow flowers in a toxic cloud.

In response to students' words, I was tossing them numbers. In response to their creative thoughts, I was totalling the cells on a rubric, where minor details were indistinguishable from major concepts. The method contradicted its objective. Grading was a miserable, unwriterly experience, and it took me a long time to grasp that it was the disjunction between the humanity of writing and the inappropriate pseudo-objectivity of the grading system that was making me miserable. I was stirring up all of this debris with my grading method, pointing at this and that and firing off minus two's and minus three's, and I was ignoring the central reality of writing. With the reality lost, the students were lost. They were just ducking and dodging the penalties I was throwing at them.

I had been thinking about the problem with professional blinders, thinking like a teacher. I finally realized that I wanted the students to do things that writers do and think like writers think, long after they are no longer students. I wanted my students to think beyond school, to pay more attention to the intrinsic core elements of writing and less attention to the additional pedagogical impedimenta—the artificial ingredients—that come with learning this process in school. If I wanted my students to become writers, I had to start thinking like a writer, teaching like a writer, and grading like a writer. How would a writer respond to their papers? Would a writer have graded their papers with schooly number deductions or rubrics? No.

In the long view, it would matter little what a student got on a nine-week grade. The details of the report card would be forgotten, but the student could move into the future with a sense of essay structure, its purpose, its lean aesthetic. I needed to pass that like a baton in a race. The trick would be to think about writing in terms of the students' next decades, to discard everything that need not be carried on.

I realized that a real writer would take this long view, would think in fundamental, literary ways about student papers. A real writer would still care about English errors, but the focus would be on the natural ingredients of writing. There would be lots of whys. There would be a different vernacular, a different tone, a different face-to-face.

So here is the method I developed, after much soul-searching and many dead ends, for grading research papers. I used it for many years, in various schools, in English and history courses, and at both middle and high schools. As I write this book I am now using it in upper elementary and middle school grades for writing courses that I teach online. This is, by far, the most successful method I know. It takes time, but it is real; it feels good and right, and I do not think it takes much more time than the old orthodox method. It does require us to have computer skills and a solid knowledge of the elements: grammar, punctuation, essay form, and MLA standards, but we should have those anyway if we propose to assign academic papers. It may not be perfect for everyone; you may need to adjust it for your circumstances, but this method works.

88

John,

If it were not for some problems in your essay structure and paragraphing, this paper would have received a solid A because it is a very impressive paper, intellectually. Your basic English is excellent; I only found one punctuation error and one misplaced modifier--no other basic errors. You also did an outstanding job adhering to the MLA standards, and your Works Cited page was perfect. Even more impressive, your thesis about Albert Camus's influence on modern literary sensibilities is superb. It is one of the deepest, most insightful treatments of any thinker that I have read this year. What this means is that when you get your essay and paragraph structures under control, you are going to write outstanding academic papers. This paper shows that you have the talent. So let us

Four-Level Assessment: English, MLA, Essay, Idea

Four-level assessment simplifies the grading of academic papers by collapsing the process down to four concepts that real writers use: the English, the format, the essay and paragraph structure, and the idea of the paper. The method accounts for the academic world's need for grades, but it introduces no artificial pedagogical devices or mathematical schemes. The assessment should not be excessively strict; there are many student errors that should be explained without deductions because they are the elements students are supposed to be learning. The goal of the assessment is to make the student feel proud of having accomplished something advanced, to feel confident about mastering the method, and to feel ready for the next level of accomplishment.

The grade of the paper is determined by assessing the quality of four dimensions, and each of these dimensions is an authentic element of good writing.

Level One: English: This is an assessment of the standard English in the paper, and *it must be acceptable if the paper is to pass*. Is the paper free of grammar and spelling mistakes? Are any mistakes that are present understandable in light of the grade level of the student, or are they sub-grade level errors that should have been eliminated years ago? Does the student adhere to grammar-based academic punctuation rules? Are there spelling errors? Spelling errors are particularly egregious in an assignment such as this because computers have spell checkers, and students have time to check any word they wish to check. (Students with dyslexia and other spelling difficulties should be invited to secure whatever support they need for proofreading the spelling; it is not a form of cheating for a student to get spelling help.) Does the student follow the style guidelines I provided, such as the avoidance of first person, contractions, and colloquial language? If there are one or two errors per page, that is one thing, but if there are five or ten elementary errors per page, that is not acceptable. If the paper is to receive a D or higher, the English must be approximately at grade level or higher.

Levels Two through Four: Each of the three is worth one letter grade.

Level Two: MLA Format: Level two is an assessment of the research paper format. In my courses, I always required the MLA method, the method of the Modern Language Association. It is the most widely used research paper standard in the world. I gave the students elaborate MLA instructions and pointedly refrained from making any personal modifications to the MLA format, insisting that students do it by the book. You should purchase the *MLA Handbook* for reference, and you will also see elaborate MLA instruction and example pages in my *Advanced Academic Writing* series. The day that papers were due, I refused to accept any paper that was obviously not MLA; I simply handed it back to the student and said that I was only collecting MLA papers, *as I had told them I would do*. Students then had to redo their papers until they adhered to my instructions, and the late penalty was one letter grade per day. Again, I do not expect that the MLA details be perfect; this is part of what I plan to teach, after all. I do, however, expect the paper to be double-spaced, with a one-inch margin all around, with long quotations indented ten spaces, with parenthetical documentation correctly implemented for long and short quotations, and with a good Works Cited page. When I calculate the final grade of the paper, acceptable MLA format counts as one letter grade.

Level Three: Essay and Paragraph Structure: Level three looks at the organization, structure, and continuity of the essay. Does it have a three-part structure with an introduction, body, and conclusion? Does it have a single thesis that ties the whole paper together? Are the quotations appropriate and relevant to the thesis? Are the sections of the body in an intelligent sequence? Do the paragraphs have topic sentences and bridges back to the previous paragraph? Are the sentences within the paragraphs organized well? Does the whole essay seem unified and continuous, or is it broken, disorganized, repetitive, or difficult to follow? Does the paper have a true conclusion that ties the parts of the body together and extracts the essence of the thesis from them? Is the thesis clearly visible all the way through the paper? Again, I do not expect the paper to be structurally perfect, but I do expect it to be a true essay and to be organized in its sections, in its paragraphs, and within its paragraphs. When I calculate the final grade of the paper, essay structure is worth one letter grade.

Level Four: The Idea: The fourth dimension of the paper is the idea, the thesis, which is the paper's reason for being. None of the other elements counts for much if the paper is not worth reading. Is the thesis meaningful, or important, or original, or creative, or enlightening? Is the thesis boring, obvious, or irrelevant? Does the paper tell us something we do not already know? What is the quality of the quotations selected? This dimension is substantive and intellectual, and it gives us an opportunity to inspire students who have never been praised for their intellects before. By congratulating students on their thinking, we make them more excited and confident about thinking; we put them in a state of looking forward to the next paper. This is the most transformative dimension, and it is the one that suddenly makes all of the other dimensions meaningful in the students' eyes. The meaning and importance of their thesis, and the fact that they came up with it, is suddenly revealed as the reason why you need good English, a good format, and a good structure. This is the place where all the lines cross and spark. When I calculate the final grade, this dimension is worth one letter grade.

Calculating the Grade: You see the calculus: English to pass, and one letter grade for each of the other three elements, then adjust up or down within the final letter grade to account for details.

Example One: Susan's paper is in good English, so she has a D; it is MLA, so she has a C; her thesis is meaningful and important, so she has a B; but the essay structure is seriously flawed, so that costs her a letter grade. She will have a B. A high B or a low B? Well, there were several spelling and punctuation errors, and her short quotations were not punctuated properly according to the MLA format. It will be a medium B.

Example Two: Robert's paper was not well proofread. Every page has grammar and punctuation errors. You have to stop reading and mark errors in every paragraph. It is a shame because the other three elements are there: the paper is MLA, has a decent essay structure, and has a really impressive idea. Robert will get a high F. He will learn the hard way, which is sometimes the best way, that a research paper is different from the games he used to play of turning in bad writing because it was accepted. We will stand our ground and not accept this English from him. We will force him to proofread maturely. We will admire the good things in his paper and express strong confidence in his future papers, and the next paper will be dramatically better; it will likely be an A.

Example Three: Ellen's paper has satisfactory English, though there are a few problems. It is an MLA paper, though she made several mistakes in her Works Cited page (not alphabetized, titles of books not in italics, no periods after some of the listings, one publisher not abbreviated). The essay structure is actually quite good. The problem is the thesis: it is a cheerful, peppy expression of how great the author is and how we should all admire his novels. This will not do, and we cannot give the paper an A. What we will do is give it a D for its English, raise it to a C for MLA, raise it to a B for essay structure, and then explain in a positive and straightforward way why the thesis of the essay is not meaningful or important enough to qualify for a letter grade. What Ellen's thesis, and the tone of her treatment of it, shows, is that she has not done enough reading of quality nonfiction. She does not yet hear the sound of nonfiction. She has not read enough good nonfiction to develop any sense of what passes for a worthwhile idea. This time, Ellen was in too big a hurry to pick a thesis and start writing; she thought of the research paper as more of a pure writing (not reading) exercise; she was impatient with library resources and did not see why she really needed to sit still and read books and articles that would help her find a more grown-up idea. Ellen will get a B, with high praise for the English, MLA, and essay structure, and when she writes her second paper, she will spend more concentrated library time reading and thinking and taking notes, and she will write an impressive paper, receiving a high A.

A comment about the weight of the English component: I can imagine someone thinking that it is too severe to make the English component so important, that a student should not fail a paper just because of this one dimension. I can imagine someone trying to adjust this method so that each level is twenty-five percent of the grade, or something similar. No, that is to miss, entirely, what a research paper is. There are hundreds of assignments that take place prior to a research paper where you can be moderate about English details, but a research paper is not an assignment for teaching English grammar or punctuation. We have moved on. At some point the students have to graduate from the level of elementary writing; at some point they have to be accountable. That point is now. Basic English is not an unreasonable expectation on a research paper; it is the absolute minimum. In this assignment students have time to proofread, to ask about details before turning a paper in, to use a spell checker or even perhaps a grammar checker, to look things up. This is when students have got to take responsibility, and that is a major part of the learning. If we have to redirect attention back to elementary grammar, then the entire nature of an academic research paper experience is damaged and undermined. Now we must prepare students for challenging high school and college work. What we do is to tell students that time's up, that as of now they must get their basic English correct, and that this is the minimum we expect on a research paper. This is the next level; our concentration now must turn to the more advanced dimensions.

83

Sandra,

I have to tell you that there are some serious problems in this paper that will have to be corrected next time, but before going into that, let me tell you what you did accomplish. Your essential argument, comparing Shakespeare's Iago to Goethe's Faust and to Milton's Satan, is extraordinary. I thoroughly enjoyed your comparison, and I was particularly impressed with the quotations you chose from the three works (Othello, Faust, and Paradise Lost) to make your case. I really do not

What to do...

What I had been doing for years was reading each paper carefully, handwriting whatever marks and point deductions I was using at the time in the margins, and writing extensive comments in the margins and on the back of the paper. This method was messy, unimpressive, time-consuming, and disagreeable. When I handed the papers back, I felt apologetic and embarrassed about the appearance of the papers. The handwriting was a problem in many ways; it took up too much space and limited what I was able to say. I was turning the paper this way and that way to scribble in the margins. The result neither looked nor felt professional.

I needed a method that was more professional, and I wanted to say much more, much faster. I wanted not only to mark the errors, but to *explain* them. During a period of years, I solved the problem. First, I replaced the point systems with four-level assessment, making the grade logical and valid and understandable. Second, I replaced my extensive handwritten comments in the margins and back of the paper with a letter to the student that I typed (I can type much faster than I can handwrite) and stapled to the front of the student's paper. Third, once I had a computer instead of a typewriter, I realized that I was explaining the exact same problems, repeatedly—what a run-on sentence is, what a misplaced modifier is, how to do the MLA margins, how to punctuate the parenthetical documentation for a short quotation—and that by using the computer I could not only save time by typing instead of handwriting, I could save massive amounts of time by saving those comments I typed most often into an archive, so that the next time I found, say, a run-on sentence error, I could just copy the explanation from the comment archive and paste it into my letter to the student. This was *really* fast.

A comment archive. For years, as I worked on stack after stack of student papers, I built up my archive of comments. Often I would revise the comment to include a new twist or to improve the wording or to include another example. Eventually, I amassed an archive of comments that allowed me to do a quick copy and paste for dozens and dozens of standard errors. This allowed me to grade a student paper much more rapidly, with much less frustration, and with a major increase in feedback to the student. With the power of the archive, I could often give a student two or more pages of feedback, explaining most of the errors that appeared in the paper. When I gave the papers back to the students, they respected the work and attention I had devoted to their papers, and their parents became intensely supportive of the process.

The computer archive changed everything. Suddenly, I could comment extensively but rapidly. Suddenly, we were all on the same page. Instead of getting a messy, unprofessional paper with ambiguous and incomplete comments back, the students were getting a personal, positive, encouraging typed letter, filled with clear explanations of their errors. They were getting a simple grading calculus that made sense. They could see that every detail was directed to their future thinking about writing. They could see that the process was as much work for me as it was for them. No longer did I receive complaints from students or parents about a grade they felt was unjust.

Part of the key was the personal and positive nature of the comments. Every letter and comment was positive. In fact, the worse the problems of the paper, the more important it was to be positive, and to tell the student that despite the problems of this paper, there were clear indications that he or she would be writing excellent papers soon. I made it a rule never to scold, never to condemn, but always to explain that the errors in the paper did not indicate the student's potential. Even a bad paper can have impressive achievements, and I made a point to find those and comment on them.

Notice how the comments in the archive were created: as responses to student errors on student papers. The archive is a kind of reality check, a database that surveys the landscape of real student writing problems.

A typical letter to a student would have the following elements:
- The number grade at the top, calculated with four-level assessment.
- The student's name.
- A positive introduction admiring the good achievements.
- Explanations of errors and achievements, most pasted from the archive.
- A conclusion with appreciation and encouragement for the next paper.

In a school year students would do four research papers, one per quarter, and they would go through this complete process four times. The result was that by the fourth quarter my students were writing better research papers than I had ever seen, and they had done enough of them that they no longer thought it was a big deal. They just used it to learn deep things about good topics, and they felt proud of their work.

LETTER STAPLED TO TOP
OF STUDENT'S PAPER

96   GRADE

Erin,

Thank you for this outstanding paper on negative indignation as a theme in Jane Austen's novels. The fact that you developed that term yourself is impressive, an indication of your depth of reading. Your argument is clearly structured and very tight; I did not see a wasted paragraph or even an unnecessary sentence. Your quotations are superb, particularly the long quote from *Pride and Prejudice*. I should also add that your English is excellent; I found one grammar error and two punctuation errors. You adhered well to the MLA format standards, though your long quotations are indented nine spaces rather than the expected ten. This is an impressive paper--much better than the first one--and it makes me eager to see what you will do with your third paper after the holiday. Congratulations on your excellent writing, and let us look at a few issues that do need improvement.

Space correctly in parenthetical notation (#)
Space correctly before parenthetical notes for long and short quotations. My # mark means that you have made a spacing error in a parenthetical documentary note. Remember that spaces are language objects, just as letters are. You have to get them right. When you use a short quotation, first give the quotation in quotation marks, and skip a single space before the documentary note "like this" (Thompson 78). "Do not omit the space like this"(Thompson 78) or put two spaces "like this" (Thompson 78). See the difference?

> On long quotations, skip two spaces after the period at the
> end of the quotation before you type the documentary note,
> like this. (Thompson 78)

Avoid using *this* as the subject of a sentence.
Please avoid using the demonstrative pronoun *this* as the subject of a sentence. Use *this* as an adjective, referring to this idea, this policy, this poem. When you just say "this altered everything," there is often ambiguity, leaving the reader to wonder precisely what you mean.

A POSITIVE, MOTIVATING, SPECIFIC INTRODUCTION

COMMENTS – SOME FROM ARCHIVE

79

James,

I know you will be disappointed with this grade, but we can avoid this result in your future papers. You will be all right; we will see to it. For now, let me tell you how much I enjoyed reading your paper and how much I admire what you did accomplish. Despite a few problems, this paper is not only impressively intellectual, it reveals a depth of comprehension in you, a talent for caring about literary ideas that few students achieve. I was impressed with your analysis of Jane Eyre's strongest temptations; most students focus on her strength, but you zoomed in on those moments when it was most difficult for her to be strong. I can hardly wait for your next papers because the problems that affected this paper are fixable, and you will clearly be writing advanced academic papers soon. You have the ability to think and draw your own conclusions beyond anything that is stated in the books you are reading. Congratulations on what you did achieve, and now let us look at the things you must change to get the A's I know you will soon make.

Please proofread more effectively.
Your proofreading is only partly effective. Even though your paper is largely free of irritating elementary errors, you have still allowed a few to slip through. Yes, few is better than many, but the principle is that in an advanced class no obvious elementary error is acceptable. Please concentrate harder on proofreading.

Capitalize proper adjectives
When we make an adjective out of a proper noun, we capitalize the adjective, just as we capitalized the noun. So the noun *England* becomes the adjective *English*, and the noun *France* becomes the adjective *French*. Now you see why we capitalize the names of some school subjects and not others: "I am reading English and history." When we are discussing the works of Sophocles, we realize that the proper noun *Thebes* becomes the proper adjective

2. The Comment Archive

In this section I present each comment that appears in the CD comment archive, and comment on the comments. We approach these details not (only) as students but also as instructors and mentors, so I shall look at each comment at two levels. I believe that this will be best accomplished if done one comment per page, for serenity's sake.

My general grading process was to read each paper carefully and use standard proofreading marks to indicate the presence of problems and errors, as well as to use quick marginal comments, later expanded in the typed letter, to reinforce and acknowledge achievements. Then I would type out a letter of comments and staple it to the student's paper.

Affectively, I wanted the student to feel proud of any achievement and to realize that I actually admired it. As for problems, I always felt that the worse the problem, the more important it was that I approach from the positive side, indicating that though there were issues, there was nothing we (WE) could not solve together.

I found that I had to reset my mind before each paper. I would finish one paper, have a sip of cold water, put aside any feelings of weariness or frustration I might feel after grading for five hours, clear my thoughts, and consciously start myself looking forward to the next paper, with high expectations and as good a mood as I could muster. This stoic/zen approach made a big difference; it is easy, when you are reading your twenty-seventh paper and you encounter yet another run-on sentence or subject/verb disagreement, to feel (unfairly) that you just got through telling this student not to do those things. The fact that it was not this student does not always matter, so there is a sort of serene maturity that you must activate when you grade important student papers. You want to approach each new student with the same high expectations, fresh mind, and fair attitude.

90

Karen,

I really enjoyed your paper on Michelangelo Merisi da Caravaggio. Caravaggio is one of those artists who can be neglected in a quick or introductory scan of major artists such as Leonardo, Michelangelo, Raphael, Picasso, and others, and yet Caravaggio appears to have had a shocking level of genius--one that he never fully controlled. Caravaggio's wild and often violent personal life seems in brutal juxtaposition with the power of his artistic vision, and I think that you have made that paradox especially clear. You did proofread the basic grammar and punctuation errors out of your paper--congratulations--and you adhered perfectly to the MLA standards; I only found one small mistake in your Works Cited page. What you have not yet mastered is essay structure and function, as well as the nuances of paragraph continuity, and I think this means that your next paper will be superb. Let us look at a few of these details.

The paragraphs in your essay should be real. Group your sentences into real paragraphs. The paragraph symbol ¶ indicates the location of paragraph problems in your paper. In organized, advanced thinking, such as an essay, you cannot let your ideas wander back and forth randomly. The ideas have to be collected into a simple, comprehensible structure that someone, including you yourself, can understand. Sentences have to be separated into clear paragraphs. A paragraph is a group of sentences all about ONE THING. All of the sentences might describe an event in time order. They might explain a thought in logical order. They might present a conclusion by proceeding from concrete to abstract. But the sentences of a paragraph must be ordered, and they must belong together in the same place, like the sentences in this paragraph I am writing now. If you are discussing the theme of man versus woman in Sophocles's *Antigone* in a paragraph, then you may not include the conflict between the brothers Eteocles and Polyneices in the same paragraph, because that conflict is not about man

Comments about Essay Structure

```
Your essay is fluent and connected.
Your thesis is in sharp focus.
Your essay has a choppy organization.
Your conclusion is listy.
Your conclusion is undeveloped.
Begin a new paragraph when you begin a new topic.
The paragraphs in an essay should be real.
You must define your paragraphs' relationships.
Connect both your paragraphs and your major sections.
Focus your essay on the thesis with microlanguage.
Your thesis should be worthwhile.
```

I eventually organized my comments into categories, grouping all of the MLA format comments together, all of the punctuation comments together, all of the grammar comments together, and so forth. As time passed, I collected more comments in each category. You can see the format I used in the list above: positive or negative, general category, abbreviated contents.

I only created a comment when I encountered the same problem repeatedly. If the problem was unusual, I would simply type out the comment spontaneously, but when the problem was one that afflicted numerous students in every stack of papers, and I was having to recompose comments on the very same problem repeatedly, that is when I would save a comment. The archive as a whole, therefore, represents a kind of map of the errors students make. It is battle-tested.

Here are the eleven comments about essay structure and paragraphing that evolved during a decade or so. The general theme seems to be clarity, unity, and continuity. Let us look at the comments in some detail...

```
Your essay is fluent and connected.
I think that you have done an exceptionally good job of writing
fluently and connectedly.  You have taken the time to begin paragraphs
with sentences linking back to the previous paragraph, and you
patiently explain each idea to the reader.  That is an excellent
technique, and you should be proud of it and continue to refine it.
```

In practice I archived explanations of problems far more than I did positive comments, which I tended to write spontaneously. There was something about the problems that was more concrete and objective. When I complimented the student, I did not want the compliment to feel canned but personal and sincere. This comment about the continuity of the writing was one of the few that I saved.

Connecting an essay may seem like a basic, introductory technique, and yet it is one of the last techniques that students master. Crude and unclear connections tend to linger in student writing long after other problems have been solved. This is because the technique is not simple and concrete, like putting a comma in a compound sentence; the problem is subtle, and it depends upon a mastery of language itself. As the student becomes better read and has been exposed to excellent nonfiction, the student acquires a reader's feel for academic connecting language, and this problem begins to abate. We certainly want to praise any paper that flows well and clearly from introduction to conclusion. We want the student to feel that his or her hard work on this detail was noticed, and that it made a difference.

ESSAY

```
Your thesis is in sharp focus.
Your paper has an outstanding focus on the thesis.  This is an
achievement that results from having done many things well at the
same time: clear wording, intellectual clarity, organization of essay
components, excellence of introduction and conclusion.
```

Here is another positive comment. I would sometimes paste this and then add to it, using it as the beginning of a more thorough explanation. A sharp thesis too is an advanced achievement. Many beginning student papers either do not focus on the thesis or do not *appear* to focus on the thesis. Often the student believes that he or she has focused on the thesis and is wounded to learn that you think otherwise.

Often this seeming blur is a result of the student using synonyms throughout the paper in order to avoid repeating the same words. The solution is to teach students to use a microlanguage, a set of two or three words that capture the elements of the thesis, and then to use those same words relentlessly in the title, the introduction, in the body, in the topic sentences of the paragraphs, and in the conclusion. The microlanguage brings unity and focus to the paper. We will look at this again on page thirty-three.

```
Your essay has a choppy organization.
Your paper is difficult to read, not because it is disorganized but
because the organization is choppy.  You have chopped your main ideas
into so many small paragraphs that the reader cannot distinguish
large sections from small sections, cannot tell when a discussion of
an idea is over, and cannot tell whether there are a few ideas being
discussed in many paragraphs or there are many ideas being discussed.
Try to have some correspondence between the idea structure and the
paragraph structure and to avoid discussing a single idea in so many
small paragraphs that the visual integrity of the idea on the page
disintegrates.
```

This highlights the importance of a correspondence between the form of the essay and its paragraphs and the form of the idea or content being described is important. The parts of the essay should mirror the parts of the content; that is what drives the paragraph structure. When we write, our eyes should only partly be on the essay itself; they should also be on the world, on the part of the world we are writing about, and in the end our essay lifts its form from the shape of the content. If the content has seven components, then we might have a nine-section essay for the seven components plus the introduction and conclusion. It is not that clear cut, but you see the point. What we must not do is to disregard the world when we write, to have some formula in mind about how writing must be organized or how many paragraphs every essay should have, and then try to force reality into that form whether it fits or not.

Paragraphs, in other words, are intellectual, not graphic. I have heard reputed experts say that you should just break up a page visually every few inches to make it more readable—that sort of thing—but what you really do is more elemental: the sentences about one thing go into one paragraph, whether there are two sentences or eight sentences. A new paragraph signals a new thought about a different piece of the content. An indentation is a promise.

```
Your conclusion is listy.
Your conclusion contains many good things, but they are not organized
well, separated clearly, tied together revealingly, or expressed
surprisingly.  It reads like a list of repetitions of things you
had said already.  I want you to concentrate on the art of writing
a convincing conclusion that will impress, interest, inform, and
convince a reader.
```

Here is another idea—what a conclusion should be—that takes time to inculcate. What students first understand is that you have to have a conclusion, but at first they simply think that this is nothing but a final paragraph after the body, where they repeat what they said in the introduction. Even that is better than what sometimes happens: a cute comment and a snappy quote. Only later do many students realize that the conclusion is supposed to make something of the body; the conclusion must process the contents of the body.

It is as though an essay is a recipe. The introduction says what we are going to make. The body provides all of the ingredients. Then in the conclusion we cook the ingredients.

I had to use this comment often. Beginning students often simply repeat a list of points they have made during the essay, giving us a listy non-conclusion rather than extracting the essence of the knowledge. If you do not draw conclusions, you have no conclusion; you only have another paragraph.

See the next comment as well.

ESSAY

```
Your conclusion is undeveloped.
Please write a carefully developed conclusion.  Now that you have
shown the reader all of the evidence for your thesis, it is time
to show what the evidence means; you cannot expect the reader to
remember everything and total it up for himself.  You cannot expect
the reader to draw the conclusions; you have to do it.  Review the
most important ideas, but do not just repeat the headlines from
the body.  Do not just reiterate what you have already said.  In
the conclusion, go to a new height.  Take the time to pull themes
together, to highlight relationships, and to synthesize all of the
information into a final recognition.  Do not introduce new themes,
but show the implications and the interrelations of the various ideas
previously explored in your paper.  Remember that the conclusion
is your first real chance to discuss everything because it is not
until the conclusion that the reader has finally been presented with
everything--with all of the facts and ideas that appeared in the
body.  The conclusion must be written with patience, insight, and
artistry.  It is the single most important section of the paper.  A
good short definition of the conclusion would be: the conclusion is
the discussion of the body.
```

We say that we *draw* conclusions. That is as good a metaphor as any.   So often, students have said to me, "I'm finished with my paper. All I have to do is write the conclusion." Uh-oh. This is a red flag, warning that the student has no idea what a conclusion is. The conclusion is the *first* chance to discuss the information of the body as a whole. Not until the beginning of the conclusion does the reader have all of the facts. The body presents the mass of data, and the conclusion is where we explain what we make of the data. We must teach students to respect the intellectual primacy of the conclusion, where new things finally get said that are more important and more comprehensive than anything said in the body.

```
Begin a new paragraph when you begin a new topic.
Use proper paragraphs.  The paragraph symbol ¶ means that you should
have indented five spaces to start the next paragraph.  Be sure to
paragraph your work properly.  It is usually best to begin a new
paragraph immediately after a long quotation.
```

There is a profound difference between knowing something at an introductory level and having a full-blown appreciation of its meaning and power. One indication of the latter is that the affective domain ignites; we can learn something at a cognitive level, and we can be able to define it and list its key parts, without caring in the least about it or being dazzled by its importance. When we finally comprehend, our emotions kick in as a response, and we care. We do this all the time with knowledge, skipping over the tedious surface and missing the point of things that could transform our lives.

One thing that can transform your life, as a writer, is to understand what a paragraph is. Much of the beauty of good writing is established by good paragraphs—true paragraphs, where no sentence is a lie. The indent tells us that every sentence between it and the next indent is about the same thing, that all of these intra-indent sentences work together to express a oneness.

When the paragraphing is gorgeous, and the paragraphs are intellectually valid, and they are woven together by weaving words in their topic sentences into a continuous focus on the thesis, this is the very fabric of clarity. It is a primary reason why some students' papers seem so understandable and persuasive, and others seem confusing and disorganized.

The paragraph is a secret, hiding in the open. Our eyes keep glancing past it. The meaning of the paragraph is: we must talk about one thing at one time.

ESSAY

The paragraphs in an essay should be real.
Group your sentences into real paragraphs. The paragraph symbol
¶ indicates the location of paragraph problems in your paper. In
organized, advanced thinking, such as an essay, you cannot let your
ideas wander back and forth randomly. The ideas have to be collected
into a simple, comprehensible structure that someone, including
you yourself, can understand. Sentences have to be separated into
clear paragraphs. A paragraph is a group of sentences all about
ONE THING. All of the sentences might describe an event in time
order. They might explain a thought in logical order. They might
present a conclusion by proceeding from concrete to abstract. But
the sentences of a paragraph must be ordered, and they must belong
together in the same place, like the sentences in this paragraph I
am writing now. If you are discussing the theme of man versus woman
in Sophocles's Antigone in a paragraph, then you may not include
the conflict between the brothers Eteocles and Polyneices in the
same paragraph, because that conflict is not about man versus woman.
Separate your sentences into the paragraphs into which they belong.

I found that I had to provide a great deal of comment about paragraphs. There are many ways a paragraph can go wrong, get blunted, admit the presence of an unregistered sentence. Paragraphs, like organisms, can have serious, even fatal, internal disorders.

One of the most serious locations for disease in an essay is within the walls of the paragraph. A reader can be injured between the indents. Everything is going well, and suddenly, two sentences into a paragraph, the reader gets confused, does not understand, wonders whether he or she is missing the thread, loses confidence in the essay, thinks that the writer did not proofread adequately, becomes bored, and either stops reading or even worse, wishes to.

Within each paragraph, the sequence of sentences must be thoughtful.

You must define your paragraphs' relationships.
At times in your paper I had difficulty understanding how what I was reading
related to what I had just read. The reader needs to know the logical
status of each paragraph. Is it another example supporting what was said
in the previous paragraph? Is this a contrasting idea? Have we begun a
completely new section of the paper? How, exactly, does this idea relate
to the thesis? In beginning each paragraph, you need to write something
that will show the reader the relationship of this paragraph to the
previous paragraph and to the thesis. Like an essay, a paragraph needs an
introduction, even if it only consists of a few connecting words, such as
"Another reason Plato was condemned by Aristophanes was . . . " You might
even need an entire connecting paragraph just to clarify the relationship
between the previous several paragraphs and the following several
paragraphs.

In a tempest a lifeline only has to break at one point, and all is washed away. Essays
are much like that. They cannot survive a break in the rope.

Every essay is a sequence of pieces. Not only is there the three-piece structure of
introduction, body, and conclusion, but each of the three may be, in its turn, composed
of paragraphs. All of these pieces must be attached, or else we have the parts of an
essay but not the essay. The parts alone are not enough; they must be assembled.

We assemble a model by taking two parts, adding glue, and pressing them together.
We assemble an essay by taking two paragraphs, adding attachment language, and
when those two are attached, we attach the next paragraph.

The attachment must be clear, not to ourselves, but to the reader. It is risky to think that
the belonging of the paragraph is obvious, or that it is implied. It is almost always better
to add wording, whether it is a simple Jeffersonian adverb or an elaborate sentence, but
something to make the place of the paragraph explicit.

ESSAY

```
Connect both your paragraphs and your major sections.
When you write the paragraphs and sections of your paper, you must
write connecting sentences and phrases--usually at the beginning
of each new paragraph or section--which show the reader that you
have left the previous idea behind and that you are now moving to a
different idea that is related to the previous idea in a specific way.
You have to write both the sections and the connections.  Otherwise,
the paper is like the pieces of a model that have not yet been put
together.
```

This is another explanation of connectivity and unity. Sometimes an archived comment would not seem to fit in the letter I was writing, and I would write it a different way and save that too. I then had a choice and could use the comment that fit best.

This comment is a bit different from the previous one in that it includes not only connecting paragraphs but also connecting sections of the essay. There are times when you cannot save the lifeline with a simple word or phrase. Sometimes you are changing to a completely different section of a paper; you have a major fracture between these seven paragraphs and those nine paragraphs, and you may require an entire paragraph or more to build a proper transition. The only rule is that the structure must not collapse under the weight of the reader's mind. Write it so that it works, no matter how elaborate it must be.

Focus your essay on the thesis with microlanguage.
I think that the thesis of this paper is not focused enough or easy enough to follow. I had to look back over the paper after I finished reading it in order to remember and retrace the ideas. Remember that a thesis essay must be a self-focusing instrument: you must construct it so that it is clearly focused on the thesis; the reader must not be given the task of figuring out how things are related to each other; that is your creative responsibility. One of the best ways to focus is to use key thesis language, a microlanguage: two or three key thesis words that you introduce in the title and introduction and then continually repeat and emphasize throughout the paper. If your thesis is that Euripides was a philanthropic pacifist, then you would explicitly express the topics of the paragraphs in terms of how they demonstrate that Euripides was philanthropic or how he was a pacifist. Those two words would keep reappearing. Every paragraph should have such a thread tying it to the central thesis. You would finish by using these same key words in the conclusion.

This concept of the microlanguage—the two or three words that capture the essence of the thesis and that are repeated throughout the paper, giving unity and reference for everything in the paper—has turned out to be one of the most important concepts, from an instructional point of view, of any I have developed. Students and teachers have told me that this concept changed the way that they write, making their writing much clearer and easier to follow. "Simplify," said Thoreau.

Teach students to use this unifying microlanguage in the title, the introduction, the topic sentences of the paragraphs in the body, and in the conclusion. The microlanguage is generated by the most concise wording of the thesis itself.

ESSAY

```
Your thesis should be worthwhile.
Have an intellectually challenging thesis.  One of the marks of
a strong essay is that it has a challenge factor; it is worth
reading because it asserts a point of view that needs proving, one
that many readers would doubt.  Merely to write a paper offering a
noncontroversial glimpse of someone's poetry, or a polite review
of someone's novel, or a hands-off explanation of an well-accepted
theory is to disappoint the reader, asking him to bear with you for
no reason.  You are proving something no one doubts!  The reason a
strong thesis is enlightening is that it surprises us; it changes our
mind; it proves to us that we had it wrong; it leaves us with a new
perspective.  It is this ability of a strong thesis to challenge and
enlighten us that is the mark of a best paper.
```

It takes some experience to begin to differentiate between what is interesting and what is not. This comment must be used in a sensitive way; it must come across as helpful, as showing the student something that all students must be shown. We do not want to imply to the student, "You are not very smart." After all, when students first begin this process of learning to write a research paper, they usually arrive with very little prior intellectual experience.

In my experience more students than not have done no serious library reading. Academic nonfiction is a new encounter for them. They need time to adapt to the ascetic goodness of academic nonfiction. We want to cast the good thesis endeavor as normal and exciting, and avoid making students feel bad about their ability—and yet we do need to explain when a thesis is not up to the standard. I think this is one of the items that takes time and requires gentle and patient—but clear—guidance.

Comments about Grammar

```
You have an adjective error.  (adj)
Remember to capitalize proper adjectives.  (cap)
Please avoid sentence fragments.  (frag)
Your main word is misspelled!  (sp)
You have a misplaced modifier.  (mm)
Keep your lists and compounds parallel.  (//)
You have a pronoun case error.  (pron)
Avoid using this as the subject of the verb.  (ref)
You have a pronoun reference error.  (ref)
Avoid the adolescent they.  (ref)
Your proofreading is unsatisfactory.
Your proofreading is seriously defective.
Avoid subject/verb disagreement.  (s/v)
Avoid the OP subject/verb disagreement trap.  (s/v)
Study how the verb agrees with a compound subject.  (s/v)
Avoid spelling errors  (sp)
Avoid split infinitives.
Keep your tenses parallel.  (t or //)
Transpose.  (tr)
```

We could list dozens of grammar errors if we wished to be comprehensive, but some grammar errors appear in abundance in every stack of student papers. These errors plague student writing. In more than a decade of grading student papers, I gradually accumulated twenty grammar comments for my archive.

These are crucial problems. Academic writing requires correct grammar. Those who dispute the importance of grammar are dreaming of imaginary colleges.

```
You have an adjective error.  (adj)
I have written adj to indicate the presence of an adjective error in
your paper.  Adjectives, remember, modify nouns or pronouns.  They
are usually found before the noun or pronoun they modify (The quick,
brown fox), but they may also be used as subject complements and be
placed after a linking verb (The fox was quick).  It is an error to
modify a verb with an adjective (Crane wrote similar).  Please note
that good is an adjective, but well is an adverb: The good swimmer
swims well.
```

It is easy to underestimate the depth and importance of the parts of speech. The more we think about what the parts of speech are doing in our sentences, the more we realize their beauty and power. In this system, modification is a major function. Having an intense awareness of adjectives and adverbs not only helps quiet the incidence of misuse, it also helps the writer to become more conscious of writing with nouns and verbs first and avoiding unnecessary (wordy) modification.

The overuse of adjectives is probably more prevalent than the misuse; this is largely a result of deficient vocabulary, which is in turn a product of meager reading experience. Students who have read a great deal of quality fiction and nonfiction absorb the vocabulary that comes with such reading, and this gives them stronger nouns and verbs to use, which helps them avoid a dependence on adjectives. The reading also acquaints them with the song of adjectives; students hear from reading experience how adjectives sound in sentence context, leaving students less likely to misuse adjectives.

```
Remember to capitalize proper adjectives.  (cap)
Capitalize proper adjectives.  When we make an adjective out of a
proper noun, we capitalize the adjective, just as we capitalized
the noun.  So the noun England becomes the adjective English, and
the noun France becomes the adjective French.  Now you see why we
capitalize the names of some school subjects and not others: "I am
reading English and history."  When we are discussing the works of
Sophocles, we realize that the proper noun Thebes becomes the proper
adjective Theban.  If you neglected to capitalize a proper adjective,
I wrote cap in the margin of your paper.
```

Here is a detail that can be cleared up at once. What the explanation shows the student is the simple, obvious logic. Oddly, obvious things often go unnoticed, and the capitalization of proper adjectives is an example. You would have to grade, as I have, many stacks of papers even to believe that this is a detail students do not grasp. It almost seems beneath explaining, an insult to the student, but it is an error that keeps appearing.

The trick in such cases is to find the right words of the logic, the aha words, so that once the student sees this explanation, the problem is solved.

What it also illustrates is the peril of teaching too fast and too superficially. If we handle problems like this piecemeal and in an authoritarian delivery, simply telling students to capitalize *French* without telling them why, they will not only continue to write *french*, but they will also write *english* and *russian* because they have not acquired the logic of the principle. The why is the key; it is always the why.

Please avoid sentence fragments. (frag)
Please write in complete sentences, avoiding sentence fragments.
My proofreader's mark *frag* indicates the presence in your paper of
a sentence fragment, one of the most serious grammar errors. It
is essential, in a formal research paper, to write in complete
sentences. There must be a subject, a predicate, and a complete
thought in every sentence you write. Common types of sentence
fragments include: 1) Dependent clauses punctuated as though they
were sentences: "When Melville went to sea. His real adventure
had begun." 2) Participial phrases punctuated as though they
were sentences: "After deserting the ship. Melville lived among
cannibals." 3) Verbless subject and appositive clusters: "Herman
Melville, a seafaring author." 4) Subjectless predicates: "Melville
arrived. Went to the Inn." 5) Groups of confused words: "Melville
in the seafaring adventure cannibals." 6) Fragments caused by using
quotations in a way that fails to complete the thought: "Spencer
believed that social struggle 'for existence as leading to the
perfect society.'" 7) The "being" fragment, in which you mistake
the word "being" for a verb: "Dante described nine circles of the
Inferno. The first circle being Limbo." Again, the fragment is
a serious error. You must write in complete sentences, not in
fragments of sentences.

The sentence fragment is one of the most destructive errors a writer can inflict upon a paper. A fragment stops a reader cold and calls the quality of the entire paper into question—deservedly so. This comment shows the student many forms of fragment; what they all have in common is that they are fragmentary, and that is the idea that must be transmitted.

Looking at this comment makes us realize the importance of level two of grammar, the parts of sentence. When we teach the nature and structure of the sentence, we must teach effectively.

```
Your main word is misspelled!  (sp)
Spell your main words correctly!  A surprisingly common--and
embarrassing--error is to misspell a key word in the paper.  An
example would be to misspell Shakespeare Shakspeare in a paper about
Shakespeare, to spell Iliad Illiad, to write a paper about Thoreau's
Walden and spell it Waldon, to spell the name Alghieri in a paper
about Dante Alighieri, or to write a paper about Jonathan Swift and
spell his name Jonathon.  In your paper you have misspelled your main
word!  It is easy to misspell the main word because it never occurs
to you that you could do something so silly, and so you do not check.
It is also common to make a spelling error in the title of the paper
or in the first paragraph because it never occurs to you that you
could make a spelling error so soon!  Always double-check these
details.
```

It is almost impossible to believe that this is a common error. Would a student really spell *Shakespeare Shakspeare* or *Sheakspear* after reading that word in source after source during a long research process? Yes. The answer is yes. Main word misspelling is a shockingly common error. I have read papers that have been so thoroughly proofread that the *only* word misspelled was the main word.

The problem arises from a sort of sleight-of-hand of consciousness; it just never occurs to the student that he or she has misspelled the main word of the paper. It is the one, the only, word that the student does not check twice. There is a blind spot, right there.

This is an error that we can have a little fun with and still correct. It is mainly a matter of reminding students that this is a common problem and teaching them to double-check their main word.

You have a misplaced modifier. (mm)

Avoid misplaced modifiers. My *mm* mark means that you have a misplaced modifier, a serious error in grammar. You must develop a sense of modifier placement. Words, phrases, and even clauses that act as modifiers must be placed next to or as close as possible to the things they modify. If you put the modifier somewhere else, it will modify something else, and the result is often nonsense. Some examples: If you say that "In an effort to be modest, Whitman's first edition of poetry lacked his name," that means that the book, not Whitman, was being modest--a ridiculous idea. To correct the modification error, place the modifier next to the word you really intend to modify: "In an effort to be modest, Whitman omitted his name from the first edition of his poetry." The sentence, "An idealist, most of Plato's ideas are only ideals" means that ideas are idealists! Better would have been, "An idealist, Plato regarded his ideas as ideals." An introductory participial phrase always modifies the grammatical subject of the sentence, and a mistake in this can result in a ridiculous sentence: "Feeling alone and desperate, this was one of Dinesen's last letters" means that a letter felt desperate. Correct would have been, "Feeling alone and desperate, Dinesen wrote one of her last letters." If you say, "Whitman got to know omnibus drivers and ferryboat pilots at an early age," this could mean that he met very young drivers and pilots. If you put the modifier where it belongs, you get, "At an early age, Whitman got to know omnibus drivers and ferryboat pilots." Modifiers are like lights; they glow on words beside them, and so you have to put them next to their intended targets.

Once again modification is a potential problem. We want students to think about modification at all levels: simple adjectives and adverbs, prepositional phrases, participial phrases, infinitive phrases, adjective clauses, adverbial clauses—whenever there is any kind of modification, the object of the modifier must be clear. Systems require connections.

```
Keep your lists and compounds parallel.  (//)
Keep lists and compounds grammatically parallel.  My mark // means
that you have a parallelism error.  Lists and compounds need to be
written in parallel form.  You could list adjective, adjective,
and adjective.  Or you could list noun, noun, and noun.  But
you should not list noun, noun, and adjective.  You might list
three prepositional phrases: of the people, by the people, and
for the people.  If you use a preposition in the first item, use
it throughout.  If you use the same preposition twice in a list,
then use it the third time also: "Socrates is mentioned in Plato's
Dialogues, in Aristotle's works, and in Xenophon's works."  Compounds
should be treated the same way; the compounded elements in compound
subjects, direct objects, or subject complements should be parallel
in grammar.  It would be wrong to say, "I like to think and
swimming."  Make it parallel: "I like to think and to swim."  Use two
infinitives, or use two gerunds, but do not compound an infinitive with
a gerund.  You must also use parallelism when you use the correlative
conjunctions: We seek not only TO be more virtuous, but also TO
fulfill our hopes of happiness.  If you use an infinitive on the left
side, then use an infinitive on the right side, too.
```

This is another error that is easy to correct. The problem is impressing it sufficiently on the student's awareness. There are many problems that students can identify, after we have called their attention to them. How do we get students to think about such problems when they are writing and to correct the errors when they are proofreading?

I think it helps to understand the problem at a deeper level, at an affective or aesthetic level. In this case making grammar parallel is like straightening books on a shelf, or arranging ornaments so that they all face to the front. It is a kind of straightening up that makes ideas easier to look at, clearer, simpler.

```
You have a pronoun case error.  (pron)
It is important to apply the rule for pronoun case: a subject is a
subject and an object is an object.  In other words the subject of
the verb and the subject complement both take subject pronouns, but
the direct object, indirect object, and object of preposition must
all take object pronouns.  Example: Freud thought a male child felt a
rivalry between him and his father, not between he and his father--
the object of preposition must use an object pronoun.  We would also
use object pronouns for objects of gerunds, objects of participles,
and objects of infinitives:  Meeting you and me was his primary
purpose.
```

Grammar is a system of systems. The pronouns are a system unto themselves, with different kinds that can be in or out of agreement, creating a risk of broken logic. That is the issue, not simply that there is a pronoun error for some reason that we do not grasp, but that there is a pronoun error in a way that is logically disturbing—a cracked thought.

The most obvious example is an error involving subject pronouns (I, you, he, she, it, we, you, they) and object pronouns (me, you, him, her, it, us, you, them). To absorb this deeply enough, we must realize that these pronouns are not just *called* subject and object pronouns, they *are* subjects and objects.

Subjects and objects are profoundly different, no matter whether they are nouns or pronouns. The subject is the hero of the sentence. It is what the sentence is about; the sentence is the subject's world. All of the objects are only that: objects in the subject's world. The eyes of the mind are always looking at the subject, and so it is potentially disturbing to see an object pronoun in a subject's place: Him is here. Or conversely: It is for I.

```
Avoid using this as the subject of the verb.  (ref)
Please avoid using the demonstrative pronoun this as the subject of
a sentence.  Use this as an adjective, referring to this idea, this
policy, this poem.  When you just say "this altered everything,"
there is almost always ambiguity, leaving the reader to wonder
precisely what this is referring to.
```

The concept involved here is pronoun *reference*. To what does the pronoun refer? Pronouns are inherently disconnected from what they replace. *This* could be anything, and *he* could be anyone, and *it* could be whatever. We love pronouns because they speed ideas up, but they do that at the risk of losing clarity.

The demonstrative pronoun *this* is a favorite of students; they use *this* to follow a paragraph and refer back to an idea in that previous paragraph efficiently, but almost always, instead of saying "This rapidly became a problem," the student will be clearer by saying, "This reluctance on Jane Austen's part rapidly became a problem," and that way the idea has no ambiguity.

Teach students to use *this* as a demonstrative adjective rather than a demonstrative pronoun, unless there is no possible reference problem. See also the following comment.

You have a pronoun reference error. (ref)

Make sure your pronoun references are clear. My *ref* mark means that you have made a pronoun reference error. Remember that pronouns are designed to be universal, and that therefore you must take pains to insure that their references to specific nouns are clear. Always ask yourself, he who?, she who? his who?, our who? who are they?, what is it? Especially when you have mentioned several different persons, the use of personal pronouns is risky because there might be antecedent ambiguity as to which of the persons is indicated by the pronoun: "Epictetus spoke of people who expressed conceit towards others, but in doing so they lost self-control." Which they? It is also easy to make a missing antecedent reference error in which you use *it* or *this* before you have even mentioned anything *it* or *this* could refer to! In fact I recommend that you never use *this* as the subject of a sentence; only use it to modify a noun subject: "This style made Dickens famous"; that is better than "This made Dickens famous." Another reference error is the talking document: "In that essay it talks about" or "In this discussion it says"; essays do not talk, authors do. Use a proper noun author's name in place of the third person singular pronoun *it*: "In his essay Octavio Paz argues . . . "

As I encountered more and more pronoun reference errors in student writing, I gradually added to the examples and categories in this comment. After several years the comment developed into this elaborate explanation of pronoun reference errors. Even this is not comprehensive.

The subtle error that I named the *talking document* is common. It is a place where conversational English washes over into the paper. As students continue to write papers and do new research with strong nonfiction, they will gradually gain a stronger command of their sentences.

```
Avoid the adolescent they.  (ref)
Make your pronouns agree with their antecedents.  My ref mark means
that you have a pronoun reference error, in this case known as
the "adolescent they," which is a disagreement in number between
a pronoun and its antecedent.  Remember that you may never use
the plural words they, them, themselves, or their to refer to an
individual or to something that is singular.  If you mean something,
someone, no one, nobody, somebody, anyone, everyone, everybody, each
person, every person, an individual, or any other singular reference,
you may not use the plural pronoun.  A person is not they; a person
is he or she.  Someone did not drop their book; someone dropped his
or her book, or someone dropped a book.  Their refers to them, and if
they are not who you mean, do not imply that it is theirs!  Please
note that even plural-sounding indefinite pronouns such as everyone
and everybody are really singular, since they emphasize every-ONE.
This is tricky when you first learn it, but learn it.
```

You see that I developed a variety of pronoun comments that overlapped. They tended to explain the same general principles but to shift emphasis to different points. The *adolescent they*, a term developed not by me but by Roy Copperud, is an especially egregious error in student writing. The problem in this case is that the *adolescent they* is a near-universal usage in spoken English. Society reinforces the error, so we must correct this error in an emphatic tone.

```
Your proofreading is unsatisfactory.
There are degrees of proofreading.  Your proofreading is only partly
effective.  Even though your paper is largely free of irritating
elementary errors, you have still allowed a few to slip through.
Yes, few is better than many, but the principle is that in an
advanced class no obvious elementary error is acceptable.  Please
concentrate harder on proofreading.
```

Proofreading is a function of how much grammar students know, and whether or not they know the grammar-based punctuation rules, as well as other concerns about the structure of the essay and paragraphs and the MLA standards.

It often takes students a number of papers to grasp what it means to proofread. At first, students tend to proofread rapidly, almost at the speed of reading, taking in entire sentences and paragraphs at a conglomerated glance and not looking pickily at the details within the sentence. Most errors, however, are smaller than sentence-size; they are hiding in the internal crannies of the sentence, and so academic proofreading is a different kind of reading. You have to proofread one word at a time, one punctuation mark at a time.

Another problem is the tendency of students to look at something, know that they are not certain about it, but rather than take the time to look it up, just say, "I think that is right." Be advised: if you *think* it is right, it is wrong. Great students become intense proofreaders; they develop a sort of elite commando attitude, forcing their way into the little details with gritted teeth, refusing to get caught with an elementary error. It is, and should be, a matter of pride.

```
Your proofreading is seriously defective.
I am sorry to have to emphasize that this paper shows a serious lack
of editing and proofreading.  You simply have not taken the time to
perfect the details of spelling, punctuation, or grammar.  You must
understand that proofreading is not a brief concluding activity; it
is a methodical, detailed, time-consuming, professional process in
which you completely rid your paper of elementary errors.  You will
have to change your proofreading methods if you are to write polished
and advanced papers.  Whatever method you are presently using to
make sure that your paper is ready to turn in, stop doing it, and do
something radically different.
```

Advanced proofreading is one of the supreme differences between advanced writing and inadequate writing. Perhaps the single element that most demands student adjustment is time, a sense of time, a willingness and expectation of careful, meticulous inspection of each word and punctuation mark. Sometimes a severe grade is the wake-up call that a student needs; it is not that the student cannot turn in a correct paper, it is that the student has been getting acceptable grades for sloppy papers. In my experience students who had seemed unable to get things right miraculously became able to get them right once I gave F's for bad English. They could do it; they just did not elect to spend the time it takes.

Part of this equation is that we as teachers must make sure that we know all of the grammar and the grammar-based punctuation rules ourselves. In the grading process we are in effect proofreading the students' papers in order to check their proofreading.

```
Avoid subject/verb disagreement.  (s/v)
Always make your verbs agree with your subjects.  My mark s/v
indicates subject/verb disagreement, one of the most serious and
embarrassing errors of grammar.  Remember that your verb must always
agree with, and ONLY WITH, the subject of the sentence--no matter
what else comes between the subject and the verb, such as intervening
adverbs and prepositional phrases that make you forget what subject
you are matching your verb to.  Also remember that certain pronouns--
such as each, someone, somebody, everyone, and everybody--are always
singular and require singular verbs: "Each of his stories contain
some philosophical view."  Each/contain should be corrected to Each/
contains.
```

Here is a focused comment about subject/verb disagreement, the worst error in grammar. It strikes at the heart of the sentence and creates a logical contradiction where there should be a perfect harmony—between the subject and its verb at the sentence's center. If you make a pronoun error, I may know that you made the error, but I will still understand you. If you make a subject/ verb contradiction, it may be fatal: dog/bark. If you say that "The dog bark," I do not know what you mean. You might have been saying that the dog barks, or you might have been saying that the dogs bark, but I cannot know from the sentence itself. The s/v error is vicious.

Understanding the nature of sentence structure beyond just parroting the definition of a sentence is critical; students need not only a survey of grammar's surface, they need deep grammar. They need to descend down and see the inner structures in the sentence. At the very center is a subject in number agreement with its verb: they will both be singular, or they will both be plural. Together, they send a unified message about a one or a many. This s/v binary pair is the irreducible quantum of meaning.

Knowing grammar is like fishing in clear water; you can see the fish under the surface. When you write without knowing grammar, you cannot even see the elements you are trying to write; it is muddy guesswork.

```
Avoid the OP subject/verb disagreement trap.  (s/v)
A special s/v trap to avoid is the OP Trap.  Do not match your
verb to the object of a preposition!  See the disagreement in the
following sentence: "Dostoevsky's views on ethics is best summed up
. . ."  The intervening prepositional phrase on ethics distracts
the mind from the real subject of the sentence, views, and you wind
up saying views/is rather than views/are.  We see the same problem
in this sentence: "The tone of Aristotle's writings were different."
Tone/was, not tone/were.  The subject is not writings, it is tone.
Or: "The impact of Plato's ideas are present in the world today."
Impact/is.  Or: "Two of the major themes in Don Quixote was humor
and irony."  Two/were.  Or: "The popularity of Pasternak's political
struggles have overshadowed the quality of his novel."  Popularity/
has.  Beware of intervening material, especially prepositional
phrases; the subject must agree with the verb.  Always find the
subject as you write your verb.
     Notice that if the subject and verb do not agree, then your
sentence is contradicting itself because one is indicating that the
idea is about something singular while the other is indicating that
the idea is about something plural.  This means that the fundamental
idea of your sentence is nonsense!
```

I gradually added examples to this comment because this is one of the most common and stubborn errors. Students tend to match the verb to the closest noun, rather than with the true subject. We see here that students who do not know their grammar have little chance of avoiding this error, which emphasizes the importance of teaching the subject-verb nucleus of the sentence.

What we also see in this problem is the wisdom of putting the subject next to the verb and avoiding intervening prepositional phrases or other content that would put the two at a distance from each other.

```
Study how the verb agrees with a compound subject.  (s/v)
You have a subject/verb disagreement (s/v) caused by a compound
subject.  Remember that a compound subject joined by and is plural
because it means both: Smith and Jones write.  A compound subject
joined by or is singular because it means only one: Smith or Jones
writes.  A compound subject joined by or but that contains a plural
noun as the second subject is plural: Smith or the Joneses are here.
As a fundamental principal of grammar, the verb must always agree
with the subject.
```

The plot thickens when the subject is a compound. The key for student learning is to comprehend the logic of the agreement, that a compound such as "sticks and stones" really is plural, whereas a compound such "a boy or a girl" really is singular.

As you see, I needed several subject/verb disagreement comments to choose from. One factor is that the error is a shape-shifter that appears in various forms, with various causes, but another factor is that unlike many errors the s/v disagreement error is one of the few that is always a possibility in every sentence; there is always a subject/verb nucleus at the center of every sentence, so there is always a possibility of getting it wrong. This risk is relentless; there is no such thing as a sentence that does not require subject/verb agreement. Because the agreement issue is present in every sentence, the error occurs more often than other errors, and to make matters worse, the error is more destructive of meaning than other errors.

```
Avoid spelling errors.  (sp)
One serious problem in your paper, as you see, is that you have
numerous spelling errors, which are not acceptable at this mature
level of academic work.  It is your responsibility to use a
dictionary until every word in your paper is spelled correctly.  I
have placed the sp proofreader's mark beside spelling errors.  Please
do whatever you must to rid your papers of spelling errors in the
future.
```

I am not a teacher who gives a student an *F* for a single spelling error, though there are some teachers who do. In fact in written classroom work such as an essay exam, I am forgiving about spelling. I have sometimes given students the opportunity to come to the front of the room and use a dictionary during an essay test, just to check the spelling of a word. I am also intensely cognizant of the problem faced by students who are dyslexic and who cannot spell for physiological reasons completely beyond their control; I never want to deduct a single point from a student because of such a physiological disadvantage.

A research paper is different. In this case the student has plenty of time to proofread, to use a spell checker, to look up a word in a dictionary, and to get help with spelling—from me or from a parent—if dyslexia is an issue. There is no acceptable reason for a spelling error on a research paper.

```
Avoid split infinitives.
In formal writing it is best to avoid split infinitives, even though
we frequently hear split infinitives in conversation.  Splitting an
infinitive means inserting an adverb or other element between the two
parts of the infinitive form of a verb, such as to run: to quickly
run.  Remember that we consider an infinitive to be one word, not two;
to run should not be split.  If we take the infinitive to see, and
split it with the adverb vividly, we have to vividly see, which is a
split infinitive.  It is better to put the adverb after the infinitive:
to see vividly.  Instead of writing that Aristophanes's criticism
allowed Athenians "to not only see that he was a better writer,"
write "not only to see."  Instead of "to more wisely select,"
write "to select more wisely."  Put adverbial material outside the
infinitive, where it will not split the infinitive.
```

The point about split infinitives that can go missing from a simple dictum about the error is that the interruption dims the power of the pure infinitive. We want students to acquire a feeling about the two parts of the infinitive going together, being a unity. The split increases the syllable count, busies the expression, and lowers the voltage of a pure infinitive such as *to imagine* or *to dream*. The point is not whether one is breaking a little rule; the point is how, at every turn, to make writing stronger. Great writing consists of many small brush strokes such as this—leaving things intact, keeping things uninterrupted, keeping things parallel, keeping things in agreement, forming the entire work into a smooth and unified articulation.

```
Keep your tenses parallel.  (t or //)
Keep your tenses parallel.  I have placed the symbol t or // to
indicate a tenses-not-parallel error.  You should not change from
past tense verbs to present tense verbs, or from present to past,
unless you have a logical reason to do so.  Do not let your tenses
wander; control them.  If you are describing something that happened
in the past, such as events in the life of Sigmund Freud, then use
past tense consistently, only changing to present tense if you begin
to describe things that exist today.  Some students are drawn to the
present tense, but I recommend the use of past tense to describe the
ideas and works of writers who are no longer living.  Let the tense
you use be true.
```

If students are describing the actions of a character in a novel, then they can use present tense to describe the character: "Jane Eyre goes from euphoria to tragedy in a moment. She flees Mr. Rochester's mansion in grief." If, however, they are describing the author, Charlotte Brontë, then they should use past tense for that: "Charlotte Brontë contributed what many feel to be the finest work of the Brontë sisters, *Jane Eyre*."

We must have students think deeply about the role of time in human existence and in what way the verb tenses account for time and our perceptions of it. The other side of the problem is that beginning writers often are not tense-sensitive; their tenses wander illogically from tense to tense. Often, the mistaken tense identifications make the meaning of the passage ridiculous; it is false that Charles Dickens *likes* to write a long novel; he died in 1870. Usually a few stern complaints about this error will suffice to call the student's attention to the problem.

```
Transpose.  (tr)
My tr mark means that you have words or letters that are out of order
and that need to be transposed back into the order in which they
belong.  I would place a tr mark beside misspellings such as thier or
beside awkward constructions such as "Then became he indignant."  I
would also do this if you wrote "Alighieri Dante" because Dante is
the first name, and Alighiere is the last name.
```

Part of the lesson here is that students often arrive at the research project with little academic or intellectual background. As instructors, we are familiar with Dante and have a sense of how his name should be used, but our students may never have heard of Dante, as incredible as that may seem.

This was one of the lessons that shocked me most, that students had never—ever—heard of things I thought everyone knew. I would tell them that *Dante* was his first name, and they would look at me with that, "How am I supposed to know that?" expression.

Read, read. We learn to write by reading because writing is what readers read. Do you want to know about writing by seeing a bunch of writing? You can see academic writing in books. Simply by reading strong nonfiction, students learn thousands of details about writing. This is why research papers are so superior to pure writing exercises; the assignment forces students to do massive amounts of nonfiction reading, and that reading is the breakthrough experience that leads them to the promised talent.

Comments about Ideas

You have a challenging thesis.
Your quotations are excellent.
Your analysis of quotations is excellent.
Please analyze your quotations.
Include your own analysis.
You wrote good appositives to identify names.
You are thinking--constructing a case.
Avoid creating sentence fragments in quotations.
Avoid elementary encyclopedias and published notes.
Do not exaggerate or make unfounded claims.
Avoid self-reference.
Create a balance between quotations and your own words.
Avoid an over-reliance on one source.
Avoid confusing sentences. (??)
Identify your sources.
Avoid contradicting yourself.
You have misquoted. (quote?)
Be aware of irony.
Use past tense for past subjects.
Be careful with paraphrasing.
The sentence has its own meaning.
This sentence is vague or ambiguous.
Avoid simplistic reasoning.
Your title is inaccurate.
You have used the wrong word. (w)

A paper with perfect English, essay structure, and MLA format that has no meaningful or interesting idea is not worth reading. Students need experience and guidance finding good ideas that are not obvious, and they need practice staging the articulation of ideas at the word, sentence, paragraph, and essay level. Learning to express ideas takes time, and it takes direct and candid feedback from us.

```
You have a challenging thesis.
You selected an advanced thesis, one with difficult ideas, and that
made your paper more challenging than if you had picked something
safer.  I am glad to see you gambling and reaching for concepts that
are a bit beyond your experience.  It is especially difficult to be
clear and articulate when you are discussing abstract, subtle, or
complex ideas, and I think that you have done a good job of working
with an intellectually challenging thesis.
```

When we model our own deep excitement about ideas and knowledge in a context of high respect for the students, the students tend to imitate us and try to participate in the life of the mind as well. Students always like to show us that our high opinions of them are right, and so it means a great deal to them when we think their papers are intellectually impressive.

The caution here is that our praise must be real, not procedural. Students quickly see through the posture of empty praise. They prefer the respect of being told when they come up short; then they can trust us when we tell them that their paper is a serious achievement.

Encouragement requires an additional layer of thought on our part as we read students' papers. The comment above is one that I would sometimes use, but often I would use it as a beginning, adding specifics about what I admired.

```
Your quotations are excellent.
A quality that distinguishes your paper is your excellent selection
of material for quotation.  These well-chosen quotations lend force
and cogency to your argument.  They also provide the reader with
extremely interesting passages to read, and they show a high level of
comprehension on your part.
```

This is another positive comment that reminds us of the need for specifics. I might use this comment, but it might be the introduction of a longer comment in which I mentioned one or two quotations with concrete specifics. Without pointing to any particular quotation, the comment comes across as mere boilerplate and loses the impact it might have.

My tendency is to use the archive more for explanations of problems and to type out positive comments individually.

As for quotations, there are a number of issues, ranging from the proper indentation and parenthetical treatment of quotations, to the flow of words into the quotation, to the relevance of the quotation to its spot in the essay.

Good quotations tend to be manifestations of student comprehension; if you do not really understand your topic or the book you are using for research, you will probably not know a good quotation when you see one, so the use of excellent quotations is an important and telling achievement.

```
Your analysis of quotations is excellent.
I like the way you take the time to discuss your long quotations
after you present them, calling attention to their meaning and to the
details that you find important.  Continue to develop that; it is a
good technique for communicating your most important ideas clearly.
```

Beginning writers may assume that long quotations speak for themselves. Although that may sometimes be possible, it is often beneficial to follow a long quotation with a paragraph that digests the quotation, making sure that the reader has not missed the point. Often the following paragraph benefits from short snips, one- or two-word requotes pulled down from the long quotation. These requotes do not need to be cited because they are in immediate juxtaposition with the cited long quote, and it is clear that the purpose is to explain.

The larger goal is to teach students the danger of assuming, particularly of assuming that they can skip small bits of work. The tendency for students is to assume that they do not need to take extra steps in the name of clarity. They assume that the path of least resistance is fine. More experienced writers assume the opposite; they assume that they cannot be in a hurry or leave pieces of ideas lying in shadowy assumption but must take the time to fit every piece into the puzzle. Taking the extra trouble to follow a quotation with a bit of explanation is one of those things that advanced writers learn to do.

The more students begin to understand the importance and power of quotations, the more enthusiastic they become about the preliminary reading and research stage of the process.

```
Please analyze your quotations.
One technique I would like you to develop is the analysis of
quotation.  In other words, you need to follow a long quotation--and
sometimes a short one--with a comment because you cannot assume that
the meaning of the quotation has been obvious to the reader.  The
reader might not have understood the significance of the quotation,
so you cannot just quote and go.  Though it need not be a rigid
(boring) pattern that you follow mechanically, you should frequently
use a three-part structure in presenting quotations.  First,
introduce the quote with a sentence or paragraph that the quotation
will illuminate, develop, or verify.  Second, present the quotation,
properly edited if necessary with [brackets] to show insertions
and . . . ellipses to show deletions (we edit quotes to remove
irrelevant material and to make the language flow well from text to
quote).  Third, follow the quotation with a comment, explanation, or
analytical breakdown of the quotation.  The comment will often use
short requotes, snipped from the quotation, to highlight important
ideas.  These short requotes should be placed in quotation marks,
but they may be freely used without parenthetical documentation,
since the documentary note has already been given in the full quote
above.  By providing this clarifying analysis after the quotation,
you can make sure that the reader understands its meaning, and you
can provide a logical bridge from this idea to the idea you plan to
feature in your next paragraph.
```

Here is the comment that explains the analysis of quotation for a student who needed to do it. There is no rule about how extensive an analysis must be; it can be any length, from a sentence to an entire paragraph or more.

The issue is the proper presentation of every quotation. Everything is important: how we lead into it, whether we insert or delete any words into or from it, how we construct the parenthetical documentation for it, and what we do at the end of the quotation to make sure that its purpose is clear.

IDEAS

```
Include your own analysis.
There is a missing element in the ideas that this paper contains.
Consider: What you have done is (1) to present examples as evidence
and (2) to present expert opinion.  You have in essence constructed a
structure that displays other people's thoughts.  What is still missing
is your own scholarly analysis of the evidence you present.  Learn
to discuss your examples after you present them, and to discuss the
opinions of experts as well.  Take the time to zoom in, to do close-
ups on the evidence.  In other words the object of research is not to
collect examples and expert opinions; it is to use examples and expert
opinions as a means of making one's own assertion persuasive.  Include
all three.
```

This comment is a shorter version of the one preceding it. No comment will always be appropriate. There are indeed assignments that do not necessarily include the student's own arguments but instead are devoted to the academic exposition of specific content. When, however, constructing one's own case is part of the possibility of the assignment, then this comment will come into play.

There is a series of steps in academic advancement that could be simplified to: presenting facts, presenting ideas, constructing ideas. At some point we do want students to acquire experience developing their own themes and insights and constructing cases for them.

```
You wrote good appositives to identify names.
I appreciate the way you wrote appositives to identify the sources of
your quotations.  On the one hand, it is disconcerting to see the names
of experts unknown to us, and on the other hand, it is informative and
clarifying to be told that an expert being cited is a scholar in a
certain field and is the author of a specific title on the subject.  You
have done a good job of informing your reader who your sources are.
```

An appositive is simply an interrupting definition, inserted immediately after the name of a person or thing, to define it at once. If I say, "Linus Pauling, the American chemist who won two Nobel Prizes, arrived for the conference," then the appositive makes the sentence clear at all points.

The appositive defines x *now*; it is the alternative to waiting until the following sentence to explain; if we wait, then the reader suffers syllables of perplexity, as long as the sentence lasts. The appositive zeros out the perplexity.

We want to teach students to favor appositives and to punctuate them correctly; appositives are supposed to be enclosed in commas, fore and aft. When the second comma is missing, there is often a disaster of meaning.

Do notice that if the subject needs explaining, the appositive may have to separate the subject from the verb, which we usually try to avoid.

```
You are thinking--constructing a case.
One of the advanced features of your paper is that the paper is not
a mere report; it is a display of your individual reasoning.  You
do not limit yourself to the role of reporter, humbly displaying
other people's ideas; instead, you structure the paper as an
argument, a display of your own ideas in which you use facts and
expert comment to support what you say.  That is excellent.
```

There are many important goals and outcomes of assigning research papers, but one of the most important is that students move beyond simply presenting unexamined facts and begin to construct their own intellectual cases, using facts and quotations to support their own ideas.

This is a level of development that most students must build up to; we often begin to see it in their third or fourth papers, after the first two papers have helped them strengthen the basics of academic language, essay structure, and MLA format.

I have devoted considerable space in the *Advanced Academic Writing* series to this aspect of student achievement.

IDEAS

```
Avoid creating sentence fragments in quotations.
When you alter a quotation by inserting words [that you enclose in
brackets] and by using . . . an ellipsis to indicate where you have
omitted words you did not need, be sure that you do so in a way that
allows the quotation to read naturally and logically, at least when
it is connected to your own words that precede or follow it.  Make
sure that the thought is still complete and not just a sentence
fragment.  In other words, do not chop the quotation up so that it
makes no sense or so that the reader has to reread the quotation to
see why it makes sense.
```

Even students who never have sentence fragments in their own text sometimes present quotations in a way that creates sentence fragments. It can happen by chopping off the beginning of the first sentence in the quote, or by deleting part of the quote, or by ending the quote abruptly...there are various ways to do it, but the quotation is a location that is prone to unintended sentence fragments.

Students need to understand that unity and continuity must continue throughout their papers, flowing unbroken even through quotations. They need to learn how to make quotations work, and a part of that is learning that they do not need to begin quoting from the first word of a sentence. A graceful lead-in might go something like:

> As Linus Pauling began to consider the complexity of the problems, he wrote in his diary that the "field around the electron exerted an unpredicted force on the other particles."

The effect of continuity is achieved by blending into the quote in mid-sentence. No ellipsis (...) is required before *field* because the quotation marks and lower case letter indicate the status of the quotation.

Avoid elementary encyclopedias and published notes.
There are several types of sources that you should not include as
sources in your Works Cited. One is the elementary encyclopedia,
such as *World Book* or *Americana*. These are not respectable as
research sources because you do not have to search for anything: the
material is pre-searched and listed in a single place alphabetically.
Furthermore, the articles in encyclopedias are written at a
universal, elementary level and only skim the surface of the subject
in the briefest way. You will not learn much there, but you might
get some ideas for real research by reading an encyclopedia article.
A second source of material that you should avoid is the *Cliffs
Notes* or *Monarch Notes* sort of pre-digested analysis. These books
are literary analysis at its lowest level and are not respected
as research sources because they are designed as replacements for
patient research. You would be far better off to seek out important
biographies and noted works of literary criticism. A final source
that you might avoid is the blurb on the slip, or jacket cover, of a
book. To quote from a slip is to suggest that you have only skimmed
the surface and did not take the time to delve inside the book.
Develop the ability to discover advanced sources of information in
the library and bookstore.

Here is a problem that is easy to eliminate. Beginning writers may not know
the difference between *World Book* and a scholarly, specialized encyclopedia of
literary criticism. They may not have seen real literary interpretation and may
think that *Cliff's Notes* is scholarly. They may be impressed with the words
on a dust jacket and want to use those without delving into the book. A good
explanation is usually all that is required to eliminate this misunderstanding.
Teach the students to find true academic sources that they are proud to include
in their Works Cited.

Do not exaggerate or make unconfirmed claims.
Beware of exaggerated claims and unsupported generalities. If you
claim that "no other author has ever" done something, what is your
evidence? Are you prepared to discuss the work of every other
author and demonstrate its inadequacy? The "most people" error
also falls in this category. If you claim that most people think
x, do you have evidence in the form of polls or statistics or even
quotations from social science that a majority of people think
x, or are you just guessing? The expressions in a formal paper
are expected to be literally true; your ideas are expected to be
accurate and defensible just as they are expressed.

The issue here is a sense of the relationship between the sentence and the truth. In daily conversation we are accustomed to loose expressions, exaggerations, hyperbole, suppositions, guesses, comparisons, metaphors, and other inaccurate, indirect, or unconfirmed propositions. Exaggeration may be what conversation likes, but it is what research avoids. In a research paper the status of a sentence is different; there is almost a part-to-part correspondence with the world. Statements in a research paper are expected to have literal truth, as though they were photographs of facts. You could almost draw lines from the parts of the sentences and paragraphs to the parts of the world that they name. The sentences are a form of data.

In conversation we glibly assert that *most people* think x or y: most people do not understand literature, most people think Alexander was a hero, and so forth. In a research paper such a sentence sets off an alarm, warning the reader that the author is not playing within the exacting bounds of academic thought. Can we trust the other paragraphs if this paragraph is undisciplined?

Avoid self-reference.

Avoid self-reference--focus on the thesis. It is important to avoid self-reference of all forms, if possible, when writing a formal paper. By self-reference I mean referring to yourself in the first person singular (I), referring to the paper itself (In this paper I intend . . .), or even referring to quotations you have presented as quotations (This quotation means that . . .). Why should you avoid self-reference? Well, when you point to something, you want a person to look at the thing and not at your hand. Mentioning yourself, your paper, or your quotations only breaks the reader's concentration by drawing attention away from the ideas and toward the paper. Do not break the spell; get the reader thinking about Sophocles, and keep the reader thinking about Sophocles.

In other words, do not unintentionally write papers about themselves; intentionally write papers about ideas.

This does not mean that you do not include your own thinking in your paper. It only means that you present your ideas without referring to yourself in the first person. You do not need to announce that it is you thinking because your name at the top of the page informs us whose views these are if they are not documented as being the views of someone else.

There is a trend in writing instruction to have students do opinion pieces in first person, but that is a bad model for what students must do in a first-quality academic paper. An academic paper is exclusively about its academic content. It is hard enough to write a paper that creates an enveloping environment of Alexander, or black holes, or Jane Eyre, without breaking the narration every five sentences with distracting references to yourself, your paper, your essay, your quotations. The trick is to write every sentence about the topic; all of the sentences face the topic, which is at the center of view.

Create a balance between quotations and your own words.
One thing you need to develop is a more even balance between the
amount of your own writing and the amount of quotation you include.
An over-reliance on either is a problem. If there are too many
quotations and not enough of your own writing, then you become too
invisible; the reader cannot tell who you are or what you think.
The main structure of the paper must be written by you and express
your ideas (without doing it in first person). The paper, in other
words, should not be a chain of quotes. On the other hand, if the
whole paper is in your own words with very few quotations presented
as evidence, then the reader will feel that you have not presented
enough researched evidence to make your thesis convincing. The
reader will doubt your ideas because you seem unable to support them.
You must construct a nice balance between writing and quotation so
that the reader sees the thoughts of your mind, supported by the
thoughts of other minds.

In first papers students sometimes rely too heavily on quotations, stringing together quote after quote with few intervening sentences of their own. The opposite can also be true, where there are few quotations, or the quotations are unsatisfactory for some reason, and the reader feels that the argument is undocumented or inadequately documented.

The research paper should not be an undocumented think-piece, and it should not be a mere book report. It should be a documented case for an idea.

Balance is probably the best word to express the ideal; I would say that a general feeling of 60/40 is about right, where the student's own words supply approximately 60% of the text and the quotations supply the other 40%. 80/20, in either direction, is out of balance.

IDEAS

Avoid an over-reliance on one source.
When most of the quotes in a research paper are from a single source,
especially if they are from only a few pages of a single source or
if they are presented in page-number order from a single source,
this gives the reader the impression that the paper is not so much
a research paper as a book report. For best effect, you need to
present the reader with diverse research evidence, avoiding the
impression that you relied too much on one or two sources.

Here is a close-up of one element of the source responsibility. Sometimes when I have assigned a paper with a minimum of five sources, a student will list five in the Works Cited page but use quotes from only one of the cited books, even from one chapter of the book.

This is almost certainly an indication that the student did not settle into the research process. Most likely, time got short and the student had to throw the paper together without adequate research, relying on one book to carry the load.

This is a serious issue that invites direct and candid comment.

```
Avoid confusing sentences.  (??)
Rewrite confusing sentences.  I have placed a "??" mark beside
sentences that are confusing to read or that make no sense.
Sometimes confusion is caused by vagueness, sometimes it is caused
by disturbed grammar or logical contradiction, and sometimes it is
caused by ambiguity (when more than one meaning seems possible).
Confusion can be the result of writing too fast, of missing words,
of trying too hard to sound intellectual, of mistakes in wording
that cause mistaken meanings, or simply of incorrect relationships
caused by imprecise statements.  Try to use the right words for
things, to avoid unnecessary words, to write with accurate details,
to include the necessary specifics, to identify the true subjects
of your predicates, and to state relationships between things with
exact language.  Read your sentence carefully; if it seems less than
perfectly clear and accurate, then edit; write it over.
```

A confusing, awkward, or ridiculous sentence is one of the more common problems in student writing. It seems to me that the essence of the problem is that students have not yet grasped the interiors of sentences and the logic that is constructed by the grammar.

The situation is often caused by writing with the mind on content rather than on the sentence. Imagine, for example, that the student is writing about the explorer David Livingstone and an encounter with a lion. Instead of thinking about the sentence itself, the student thinks about Livingstone and writes, rapidly, "Gnawing the bloody antelope haunch, Livingstone glared at the lion." This catastrophe, in which the disturbed grammar means that Livingstone is eating the meat, happens when the student does not turn his eyes from the content to the sentence. The student is not really even looking at the sentence.

IDEAS

```
Identify your sources.
It is a good idea to identify names the reader might not recognize,
especially when you are first referring to authors and experts at
the beginning of a research paper.  If the person is important to
your argument, you might write a paragraph or at least a sentence
explaining who the person is and what his or her credentials
are, as well as a brief explanation of how the expert's views are
important to your thesis.  If the source does not play a major part
in your paper, then use a briefer identification, such as a graceful
appositive after the name or a quick prepositional phrase before it.
You might say, "Ian Hamilton, author of Robert Lowell, disagrees."
Or: "In his biography Robert Lowell, Ian Hamilton candidly notes
that . . . ."  It is unsettling for a reader to be faced with
unidentifiable names, and if your source is really an authority, then
you want your reader to know why.
```

We want students to have a sense of being patient and closing the gaps in the argument. Simply naming the author of a quotation is better than presenting the quotation anonymously, but it is better to provide information that will make the person's quotation credible.

Multiple sources that agree provide an additional layer of strength to an argument. We know from the *ad hominem* error that a proposition is neither true nor false because a certain person states it; the identity of the author is not evidence, but the more scholarship we can find to support an idea, the stronger the case will be.

Having said that, I should add that intellectual history is replete with moments when predominant theories turned out to be mistaken; the consensus of experts does not establish proof.

```
Avoid contradicting yourself.
I have placed an (X) symbol to show that you have logically
contradicted yourself.  Probably you did not think contradictory
thoughts, but you have worded your sentences so that you express
contradictory thoughts.  In a formal paper it is the expression of
thoughts that is most important.  You can not expect a reader to
guess what you think.  Look closely at the passage I have marked,
and you will find that what you have actually written means the
opposite of what you meant to write.
```

Here is another comment that is really about the nature of the student's concentration. In our responses to students, we will have to come at this issue from a number of angles until students learn to look at their sentences, rather than just letting their eyes bounce from period to period.

Good writing involves multi-level awareness, and one of the most critical levels is the intra-sentence level, where the student must stop chasing after the meaning of the content, must stop and look at the insides of each sentence. The student must stop looking at the sentence and seeing what he or she means; the question is not, "what does the student mean"; the question is, "what does the sentence say."

Knowing what you mean can be the most distracting and deceiving force; there is a powerful tendency to see what you mean rather than what you have actually said. It can take students years to achieve the undistracted strength of vision that good writing requires.

```
You have misquoted.  (quote?)
I have written quote? on your paper to indicate a quotation that
seems to be flawed.  As you have written it, the quotation does not
make sense, and I think that you have made an error in transcribing
it.  Either you mispunctuated, omitted a word or words, added a word
or words, or changed words; any of these could have happened.  It is
also possible that you simply do not understand what the quotation
means, and you have unwittingly tried to place it in a context in
which it no longer makes sense.  Without seeing the page you copied
from, I cannot be sure what happened.  In the future please be sure
to copy with perfect precision.
```

Misquotes are common. The two primary causes are that (1) students do not grasp the towering imperative that a quote be exact and that (2) students who do try to get quotes right fail because errors slip in through the multiple copying process. Students have to copy from a book to their notes and from their notes to the paper, and these are the weak links.

The best defense against misquoting is ultra-careful proofreading. When students learn to proofread slowly, minutely inspecting every detail, they are most likely to spot a mistake. Students who proofread at a normal reading speed are unlikely to catch a misquote.

```
Be aware of irony.
Be wary of irony and satire in literature; a too-literal
interpretation can lead you astray.  Literary analysis is an
advanced art, and it takes time to learn to read things that have
indirect or ironic themes, where the real meaning is actually the
opposite of the one expressed.  Let me give you an example: Jonathan
Swift, the author of Gulliver's Travels, wrote an essay entitled
"A Modest Proposal," in which he argued that the Irish potato
famine should be solved by eating Irish babies!  Since there was an
overpopulation crisis in Ireland, Swift argued, and since babies
are obviously rich in protein, this efficient solution would solve
two problems at once.  Of course Swift was not actually advocating
cannibalism.  He was actually mocking the brutal indifference of the
English government that had the power to do more to ameliorate the
suffering of the Irish than they were doing.  Mark Twain was doing
something similar to this in his ironic discussions of Christianity.
He was not to be taken seriously when he said that Heaven will
just consist of everyone playing a harp and singing, things that
men despise.  What he was serious about was his contempt for the
shallow, unthinking, lazy way that some read the Bible, as though it
were a cookbook, or a farm implement catalog, with only one level
and no profound meanings whatsoever.
```

Experienced readers become familiar with various strategies of discourse, including ironic presentations that refute ideas by pretending to advocate their horrible consequences. It is not unusual in intellectual history for an author to attack a stupidity by pushing it into the light and pretending to support it. An experienced reader will recognize this as a savage attack.

The problem is, many students are not experienced readers. Their primary reading history may consist of nothing but textbooks, which are the most straight-faced and one-dimensional books imaginable. Students who come from a textbook background may be utterly unequipped to notice irony and may need our guidance as they plan their papers.

Use past tense for past subjects.

Use past tense verbs to describe the past. Though many students are tempted to use present tense in writing research papers, especially if the papers are about the works or literary ideas of writers, it is often advisable to use past tense instead. Past tense seems to be more manageable and to result in fewer tense parallelism errors, and past tense is the logical tense to use in describing an author who has been dead for centuries, such as Shakespeare. A verb's tense is part of what it predicates about its subject--part of the claim made by the sentence, and so there is something slightly jarring about a sentence such as, "Shakespeare writes his sonnets in a different sonnet form than Spencer" because we are aware that Shakespeare is not a living writer, as the tense of the sentence implies. To say that "Aristotle believes in following the Golden Mean" is disturbing to our awareness that Aristotle is dead. Strictly speaking, it is false that Aristotle believes in the Golden Mean, but it is true that he believed in it. Although we sometimes employ a literary convention that allows us to speak of dead authors in the present tense, it is perhaps best to match each verb's tense to the truth, and to speak of past events in past tense.

This version of the verb tense idea complements the other comment that I included in the grammar section. Here the emphasis is more on the fact that a tense can be true or false, part of the essential validity of the argument.

We want the student to be thinking that way about every sentence: as the sentence is worded, is it true? This includes tense. I see grammar dicta that offer authority about how to use tense, but I think the best guide is to make sure that the tense is true. It is not true that Shakespeare is a good writer.

Be careful with paraphrasing.

Paraphrasing is giving a short summary or significant rewording of someone else's work. You might paraphrase because to quote would take too much space, as, for example, if you are condensing several pages or more down into one paragraph. Or you might paraphrase because the printed passage does not work if treated as a quotation; perhaps it is too scholarly or abstruse and needs clarification. But notice that paraphrase is NOT a near-quotation. You should never almost quote by slightly changing a word here and there--this gives the false impression that you are the author of these sentences, when actually the real writer wrote them, and you have only barely modified them--a dishonest misrepresentation. If you are going to near-quote, do not; just QUOTE.

It is also often difficult to tell where a student begins to paraphrase, so when you paraphrase an idea instead of quoting it, please use the following method: 1) Begin by naming--and if you have not previously done so, identifying--the person whose idea it is. Example: In his *Story of Civilization*, Will Durant notes that . . . After you have named and identified the source, 2) paraphrase the idea until you have accomplished what you wished. When you have finished paraphrasing, 3) include a standard parenthetical documentary note containing name and page number (Durant 685). Put the period after the parenthetical note, not before it. Please understand that some instructors would not require you to name the source of your idea at the beginning, but I think it prevents confusion about which ideas are yours and which ideas are someone else's, and it completely protects you from charges of plagiarism.

Plagiarism is the monster in the house. At any moment it can leap out and wreck the place. Students must learn the dire consequences of plagiarism, and this comment about how to paraphrase is directed at providing guidelines for avoiding one form of plagiarism. The reader must always know whose work words are, including and in some ways especially when paraphrasing is involved.

```
The sentence has its own meaning.
Remember that once you make a sentence, it means what it means--
not what you mean.  If you want to add 43 and 7 on a calculator, and
you punch in 43 x 7, the calculator will give an answer of 301, not
the 50 you expected.  A sentence is just like that.  Its meaning has
nothing to do with YOUR private intentions; its meaning is based on
ITS structure and logic.  Ideas are like mathematics; the meaning
of a sentence/idea is based on the instructions contained in the
grammatical structure you construct, and if you enter the wrong
instructions, the sentence will mean something different from what you
are thinking.  The poor reader has only the sentence to experience,
and the meaning that comes to the reader's mind will be based on
the sentence--as though you did not exist.  So when you write a
sentence, you must perform a feat of advanced concentration in which
you completely silence that part of you that knows what you mean;
then you must look blankly at the sentence and change the words and
structure until ITS meaning is accurate exactly as IT is stated.  It
is the sentence that counts; it does not matter if YOUR meaning is
clear--what matters is that ITS meaning is clear.
```

Here I take another stab at asking the student to think more patiently and in more detail about the idea in the sentence. The problem of ideas extends down to the sentence level. In fact the subject/verb nucleus is the very quantum of meaning—a paper is essentially just a series of such binary structures, and so the essence of meaning emerges from the cores of the sentences. Students must learn to hold up sentences and look in there, checking not just grammar and punctuation but the idea itself.

This sentence is vague or ambiguous.
Avoid vague and ambiguous sentences. There are several ways for
the meaning of a sentence to go wrong. One is that the sentence
might be vague, which means that the sentence is unclear, nebulous,
incomprehensible. A vague sentence is one in which no clear
meaning can be deciphered. A second way that a sentence can go
wrong is that the meaning is ambiguous. This means that there are
two or more different meanings that are possible, and the reader
is unable to determine which of the possible meanings the writer
intended. Writers sometimes deliberately use double meanings to
enhance their writing, but in a formal paper, ambiguous meanings are
usually neither intentional nor desirable. Avoid vague sentences
and ambiguous sentences. The solution is to rewrite the sentence,
replacing generalities with the specific details that would have made
the meaning clear. Vagueness and ambiguity are two results of not
being specific enough, of not including enough specific details.

As you see, I eventually developed a choice of comments to use in discussing twisted sentences. Typically, I would begin with one of these comments from the archive, and then continue the comment spontaneously, discussing the particular sentence involved.

```
Avoid simplistic reasoning.
I say that your reasoning is simplistic not because you are wrong
in your essential point, but because you need to be careful about
oversimplifying, about reducing what is obviously complicated and
multifaceted into a too-easily explained answer.  You want to avoid
giving the reader the impression that you have not really looked
deeply into the issue, or have not considered all aspects of the
problem.  If the reader feels that there is obviously more to the
problem than you seem to realize, then you are in trouble.
```

This comment would be a beginning, to be continued with specifics about what part of the argument was oversimplified. This is a touchy issue that risks making a student feel stupid, which would be counterproductive and false to our feelings and intentions. It is not uncommon, nevertheless, for students to see content in a one-dimensional, black and white, beginner's way.

The problem is one of experience. As we grow older and read more, our knowledge increases, and we become aware of complexities and additional elements of experience, and the answers no longer seem as obvious to us as they once did. Beginning writers naturally have not yet seen as many sides to life as more experienced scholars have, so we have to be fair about this and regard it as natural while still pointing it out and giving guidance that feels encouraging to the student.

Your title is inaccurate.
Write an accurate title for your paper. The title of a formal paper
should be true, precise, and specific. It should be, probably, a
thumbnail expression of the thesis expressed in microlanguage,
rather than a mere general categorical term. A paper on imagery in
Hamlet, therefore, should not be titled "Shakespeare," but should
be "Imagery in Shakespeare's *Hamlet*." If a title is too broad, it
is actually false, since the paper does not really discuss what the
title promises, but only a small portion of it. Please write an
accurate title for your next paper.

Students may never have thought about the fact that a title should be the truth, but it should be. The title is a kind of promise, a label that tells the reader what is inside the box. A reader who believes the label and then finds that the contents of the box are not as advertised has a right to feel misled.

Teach the students to make the title an accurate thumbnail of the thesis so that the title is the very idea of the paper in a most abbreviated form. Ideally, the title will use the two or three words of the thesis that we referred to as a microlanguage, and these words will be used throughout the paper to provide unity and clarity.

IDEAS

```
You have used the wrong word.  (w)
Choose your words carefully.  My mark w means that you have used the
wrong word.  When you write a sentence, it is easy to use a word that
sounds impressive but that has a wrong or even absurd meaning.  If,
for example, you say that "Sinclair's family sided with the movements
of the Confederacy," I wonder what you mean.  Political movements?
Military movements?  In this case movements would seem to be the
wrong word for your sentence.  You could leave it out: "Sinclair's
family sided with the Confederacy."  Or you could change it to
something more direct: "Sinclair's family sided with the states/
arguments/opinions of the Confederacy."  Be wary of picking words for
their sound; sense comes first.
```

Here we see the element of idea and truth extended to the word level. It is not simply a question of breaking some arbitrary English rule; the issue is that the word is not true. Even the individual words should be true.

If you say that Sinclair's family sided with the *movements* of the Confederacy, then there must be movements, moving, to which you refer. If there are movements, then be specific; if there are not movements, do not use the word; instead, use a word that is true.

So much of the secret of good writing is viewing the entire enterprise not in terms of obeying writing rules but in terms of truth. Is the thesis true? Is the paragraph true? Is the sentence true? Is this word true? Wrong words are not only incorrect; they are false. Thinking of writing this way resolves many ills. It is both simpler and more profound.

Comments about MLA Format

Your MLA details are excellent.

Your Works Cited page is excellent.

Put an MLA parenthetical after each quotation.

Understand how documentation works.

Format long quotations correctly.

You may document poems with line numbers.

Please double-space your entire paper.

Avoid handwritten headers.

Follow the instructions for your header.

Indent properly. (5> 10>)

Use a ragged right margin, not a justified margin.

Follow the MLA margin rules.

Indicate mistakes in quotations. [sic]

Follow the MLA rules for the title.

Document editors correctly.

Construct your Works Cited title correctly.

Format the Works Cited page correctly.

Abbreviate publishers' names.

Use *et al* for multiple editors.

Avoid widows and orphans.

Use Courier type font, not Helvetica or Times Roman.

My choice of the available research paper formats always has been the MLA method, created by the Modern Language Association and documented by the *MLA Handbook*. It is the simplest and easiest to learn and set up for beginners, and it is a form of knowledge itself because it is the most widely used research format in the world, used by more high schools and universities than any other. We should adhere exactly to the MLA method without introducing any personal variations—we should do it by the book.

```
Your MLA details are excellent.
I appreciate the excellent job you have done of following the MLA
format.  Your title page, your documentary technique, your margins
and spacing, and your Works Cited listings all show advanced
attention to detail.  This gives me, as a reader, more time to spend
thinking about your ideas.
```

When everything is right, I use this comment to summarize the student's accomplishment, leaving me more time to help the student with problems. It is no mean feat for a student to get all of the MLA details right; MLA might be the easiest of the major research formats to use, but that does not mean that it is easy for a student who is encountering it for the first time.

A core concept here is the very nature of standards. Students do not grow up today in an environment of inflexible standards; they grow up in a culture of informal flexibility and personal preference. It can be a shock to students to realize that they are not entitled to any personal preference about research paper standards; everything must be by the book: the margins, the documentation, the line spacing, the title information—everything.

So part of the experience is the cultural shock-wave that hits the student who has never had to internalize and apply a complex system of standards.

In other words, it is outstanding training.

```
Your Works Cited page is excellent.
Your Works Cited page is extremely well done.  I appreciate the
trouble you took to study these important details and to get them
right.  This is one of the most professional and impressive features
of your paper.
```

In a paper that adheres almost perfectly to the MLA standards, the location of likely errors is the Works Cited page. This is because there are tight rules for each listing, and there are many different kinds of works that can appear. It is impossible to have students memorize every conceivable type of Works Cited listing. The best plan is to have them memorize several basic listings, understand the inflexible expectation about the details, and then look up any variation that they do now know in the *MLA Handbook*.

We want to instill a kind of reverence for the Works Cited page, to have students realize that this is the epicenter of honor in the process, the place where we enjoy crediting scholars who came before and created wonderful insights and passages. We do not want students to view Works Cited as a kind of dreary ordeal; they are participating in a tradition of honesty and academic honor that extends back for centuries.

Put an MLA parenthetical after each quotation.

Please document every quotation. In a formal MLA paper, every quotation, long or short, must have a parenthetical documentary note (not a footnote or endnote) accompanying it. The note is in parentheses and usually includes only the Works Cited author's name and the page number that the quotation is taken from. There is no comma between the name and page number. The author's name in the note links directly to the alphabetized names on the Works Cited page. If the note says (Johnson 192), then I expect to look at the Works Cited page and look down alphabetically to the J's, where I will find a book by Johnson.

For short quotations the documentary note should immediately follow the closing quotation marks, "like this" (Thompson 164). Notice that the *period comes after* the closing parenthesis.

> In long quotations, which are indented ten spaces and do not use quotation marks, the documentary note comes on the last line of the quotation, but after the period instead of before, like this. (Thompson 137)

Here is a critical detail. I had to use this comment often until students began to differentiate between short and long quotations and to appreciate fully the importance of the period moving back and forth from before the parenthetical to after the parenthetical. At first students often could not understand the big deal about the exact location of a period.

When the format is perfect, the reader's mind looks unhindered at the content. When the format is marred, there is a gauntlet of impacts on the reader's attention, distracting and obstructing his or her view of the content.

Understand how documentation works.

Tie the parenthetical notes to the Works Cited. You seem to misunderstand what a parenthetical documentary note is supposed to include and how it functions. The documentary notes simply direct the reader to the Works Cited page. In the parenthetical note, you only put a Works Cited author's last name and a page number. The reader can then flip to the Works Cited, which are in alphabetical order by authors' last names. There, the reader scans alphabetically down the names until he or she sees the *same name* you listed in the documentary note. In other words the name in the note is the same as a name in the Works Cited; you use the alphabetized names from the Works Cited to put in the documentary notes. The only time you do not do this is when you do not need to because you already mentioned the name in your text and you can just put the page number in the note, or when you cannot because you have no name, only a title. Otherwise, just put the author's name and a page number like this (Thompson 89).

One of the most common errors that students make is to put a name in a parenthetical, such as (Mallory 98), and when one looks at the Works Cited page, there is no Mallory listed. When questioned, the student pleads that he or she has listed the book under the book's author, Jones, but the quotation is by Mallory. The student has missed the point of the system.

In the parentheticals and in the Works Cited, we see the same names, twice. Each name in a parenthetical ties to itself repeated in the Works Cited.

When an instructor encounters this error, the best plan is to gasp and moan and look incredulous and express complete disbelief. Collapsing is allowed.

Format long quotations correctly.

Learn the correct MLA treatment of long quotations (more than four typed lines): long quotations should be double-spaced, should be indented ten spaces from the left margin, and should extend out to the right margin, rather than being indented on the right as well. Long quotations should not begin on the line of your own text above the first indented line, but should be entirely set apart in the indented area. Usually, you use a colon at the end of your own words to introduce the long quote:

> Long quotations should not be placed in quotation marks
> unless there are quotation marks in the book from which you
> are quoting, as in a dialogue between characters. Only
> short quotations of one to four typed lines should be
> placed in quotation marks. In a long quotation, the final
> period should be placed at the end of the quote, followed
> by two blank spaces and the parenthetical documentary
> note. The period only follows the documentary note if the
> quotation is short. (Thompson 86)

MLA does a beautiful job of formatting long quotations. Double-spacing the quotation to make it visually harmonic with the text creates a smooth visual flow from the text into the quotation. The ten-space indent distinguishes the quotation from the five-space indent of the paragraph. It is elegant and clear. The minimalist documentation in the parenthetical further reduces the formatting noise. It is clear, clean, and simple, like a Japanese interior. This quiet system allows all of the attention to be on the ideas.

MLA

You may document poems with line numbers.

For a parenthetical documentary note at the end of a quotation from a poem, you have the option of simply providing line numbers, rather than author and page number. In this case, you give only the line numbers, not the name, page number and line numbers. For example, if you are quoting from the first four lines of Sylvia Plath's "The Moon and Yew Tree," you would not list it as (Plath 27, lines 1-4), but only as (lines 1-4). This is because the lines would always be the same in every book containing the poem, or at least that is the assumption, even though some poems (such as Walt Whitman's) have gone through numerous revisions. If you are citing a poem that appears in numerous different versions, use the traditional name and page number documentary citation.

Here is another example of the elegance and intelligence of the MLA method. The details of the format have been the object of careful thought. If a student chooses to document a poem in the standard way, rather than with line numbers, that is not an error. The best plan is to be sure that students understand this option and make a choice that is appropriate for the details of the paper.

```
Please double-space your entire paper.
The MLA rules call for you to double-space your entire paper,
including the title-page information at the top left of the first
page, the long quotes, and the Works Cited page.  You should also
only double-space down from the title to the first sentence of the
paper, double-space down to and from each long quotation, and double-
space from the header at the top of each page down to the first line
of the page.  Be careful not to use space-and-a-half or triple-
spacing.
      Note that in some methods long quotes may be single-spaced, but
in the MLA method everything is double-spaced.
```

Here is another detail that distinguishes the MLA format. The method is consistent. The papers are visually uniform, being double-spaced throughout. There are no blank lines, not between paragraphs, around long quotations—not anywhere. The MLA paper looks very much like the page of a good book, which is the point.

Double-spacing is one of the elements that makes an MLA paper so readable; it removes the visual impedimenta and lets the reader's mind become immersed in the ideas.

```
Avoid handwritten headers.
Please do not hand-write your name and the page number at the top of
your pages.  If you forget to type the name and number, or if your
word processor gives you problems, put the sheets in a typewriter
and type the name and number on each page separately.  Remember that
the name and number should be only one-half inch below the top of
the paper, and flush with the one-inch right margin.  From there, you
double-space down to begin your text.  This will give you a one-inch
margin at the top of your page.
     Remember also to set the header in Courier, just like the rest of
the paper.
```

This comment is less relevant than it once was, now that typewriters are extinct and word processors are easy to use. I am leaving it in the archive as an illustration of problems that can arise when a student cannot control the details of the word processing software.

This does happen. I have often had students phone me to ask for help when they could not make their word processor do what I had said was required. As software has become more consistent and simple, the problem has abated.

Typically, the header problem is addressed through a header function in the word processor. One typically inserts a header, then types the last name into it, then a blank space, and then a command such as "insert page number" from a menu of commands. You may have to make sure that the header is in the same type font as the paper.

```
Follow the instructions for your header.
Make your page headers correctly.  Please study the MLA page-
numbering method.  Using Courier type font flush right, you should
type your last name, followed by one blank space and the page number:
Smith 3, at the top right hand corner.  Notice that you do not use
the word "page" or its abbreviation.  Notice that you do not put your
name in all-caps: SMITH 3.  Notice that you do not omit the blank
space: Smith3.  Notice that you use numbers, not Roman numerals.
Also notice that there is no punctuation, such as a comma, between
the name and page number: Smith, 3.  Your name and page number should
be in the top right-hand corner, only one-half inch below the top of
the page and flush with the one-inch right margin.  From this, you
double-space down to start your text at the one-inch margin; in other
words, there is only one blank line between the header and the first
line of text, not two.  Sometimes, students use their first initial,
followed by a period, before the last name.  This is acceptable.  The
header should look like this:

.........................top of page.........................
                                                        Smith 3
This would be the first line of your own text.  There is only one
blank line between the header and your text.  See?  The header is
one-half inch down, and the first line is a full inch down.
```

I have seen students get the header wrong in every way imaginable, even though I always explain in detail what to do. You will see in the comment many of the bizarre variations of errors that have occurred.

If the student gets the header wrong, there is no remedy other than a gnashing of teeth. Smiting of forehead is acceptable as well, so long as the forehead is one's own.

```
Indent properly.  (5> 10>)
A 5> or a 10> mark means that you should have indented the paragraph
five spaces or the quote ten spaces.  In accordance with the MLA
instructions, we put exactly five blank spaces at the beginning of a
paragraph, and we start typing on the sixth space.  We put exactly
ten blank spaces before each line of a long quotation, and we start
typing on the eleventh space.  The second line, not the first, of each
Works Cited listing should be indented five spaces.  You can indent by
hitting the space bar repeatedly, but it is easier to set your tabs
at the fifth and tenth space.
```

The standard is five or ten spaces; it is not four, six, nine, or eleven. There is something about this standard that can seem beneath concern to students who think in approximations. I have told them five or ten, and they turn in four or nine, and they are astonished when I mark their errors.

Sometimes this problem is caused by a student using the built-in tab feature in a word processor. The student gets to a new paragraph, hits TAB, and begins typing, assuming that the default tab will be in accordance with the MLA requirement. Alas, not all default tabs are set at five or ten spaces. Sometimes they are set at one-half inch, and this may or may not mean five spaces, depending upon the size and style of type used.

This comment also brings up the strong advantage of using Courier type font; Courier is a monofont in which all letters take up the exact same width, making perfect spacing and tabbing easy and visible. Courier makes both the student's and the teacher's jobs easier.

```
Use a ragged-right margin, not a justified margin.
Use a ragged-right margin.  Please do not justify the right margin
of your paper.  Instead, use a ragged-right margin, set  one inch
from the right edge.  Even though a justified margin is beautiful to
some people, it distorts the spacing of words within the lines, and I
cannot then tell whether or not you have made spacing errors.
```

This comment is directed at the instructor's ability to grade the spacing of a paper. A space is a language object, just like a letter. The writer is expected to put one blank space between words, and usually two blank spaces after the period at the end of a sentence (although MLA now makes one space optional, at the discretion of the teacher).

A computer justifies lines by stretching or shrinking spaces between words, and so when a student justifies a paper, it becomes impossible for the instructor to see if the spaces are correct.

By requiring flush-left Courier, the instructor will be able to see whether the sentences are spaced correctly.

Notice that ragged-right is more readable; the curves of the right margin give visual guidance for the eye.

Follow the MLA margin rules.

Please observe MLA's one-inch requirements for margins. You should
have a one-inch margin all around the paper, except that the name
and page number (the header) at the top right-hand corner of the
page are set only one-half inch below the top of the page. Double-
space down from the name and page number to begin your first line,
and you will have a correct one-inch top margin. Please notice that
the one-inch right margin includes long quotations; even though long
quotations are indented exactly ten spaces from the one-inch left
margin, they are not indented from the right margin. See the sample
pages in the *Advanced Academic Writing* texts.

        Please use ragged right. Note that in an MLA paper the right
margin will not be at exactly one inch for every line, since you are
using a ragged-right setting rather than a justified setting, which
stretches or compresses the lines so that each line ends exactly at
the right margin. In a ragged-right setting, only the longest lines
extend out to the one-inch right margin.

Here is another element of the simplicity and clarity of the MLA method.
Just as the whole paper is double-spaced, the whole paper uses the same right
margin. There is a smooth visual consistency that also makes the writing
simpler, subject to fewer shifts and changes.

```
Indicate mistakes in quotations.  [sic]
If there is a misspelling in a quotation that you are including, you
may insert [sic] in brackets (do not use parentheses) immediately
after the misspelling to indicate that the misspelling is part of the
quotation and not your error.  This word sic is the Latin word for
thus and means that you found the quotation thus.

     Do not overuse [sic] by inserting it after every idiosyncratic
punctuation, British spelling, colloquialism, or archaic spelling.
It will be obvious to the reader that such things are part of the
quotation.  You need only insert [sic] when there is a true spelling
error in the quotation.  Think of it this way: use [sic] if there is
a publisher's typographical error in the book.  If it is not a typo,
and the book is printed the way the publisher wanted it, you usually
do not need [sic].
```

The graceful, correct, appropriate, and effective use of quotations is one of the advanced elements of writing. It can take a few years and five to ten papers for a student to get good at using quotations. Here is one of the more concrete and teachable details of quotation use.

Part of the problem is that quotations are inherently zones where errors are likely. Students often copy quotes to their notes, and then copy from their notes to the paper, and each step exposes the quote to intrusions and omissions. Students often make mistakes when they copy from a book to their notes; they misread or fail to notice small details of punctuation. Students also often do not proofread their quotations as carefully as they read their own text; why should they, when the words are directly from a book? We have to teach students that every quotation is a bed of quicksand.

Follow the MLA rules for the title.

Construct your title correctly. Please review the MLA requirements for the title of the paper. The title should be exactly centered, should be double-spaced, should not be in ALL CAPS, should have the First Letter of Each Major Word--but not prepositions, conjunctions, or articles--Capitalized, and should not be in italics, unless you use italics to indicate a book title or something else that belongs in italics. (In the past we underlined book titles, but the new MLA standard is to use italics instead.) You should only double-space down to the title from the date above, and you should double-space down to the first paragraph from the title. If you use both a title and subtitle, use a colon and one blank space between them: H.G. Wells: Master of Science Fiction. If the title takes up more than one line, break the title at an appropriate mid-point, rather than have just one word or two on the second line, and double-space between the two lines of the title.

Here is another comment that lists many ways a student can go wrong. When I began assigning research papers, it never occurred to me that the simple title would be a crash zone, but I slowly realized that the title was one place where errors are most likely.

I think that at first students just do not hear the standard. They just think about the title in a personal way: "Here is the way I like to do my title." It can take a paper or two to make students realize that there are standards governing the exact treatment of the title, and that personal preferences are not acceptable alternatives.

Document editors correctly.

Learn how to document a book editor in a Works Cited listing. When
the name that begins the listing is the name of an editor rather than
an author, then you indicate the editor by abbreviating this way:

   Jones, Susan, ed. *The Power of Poetry*. New York: Simon,
      1992.

If the editor's name appears inside the listing instead of at the
beginning, then you indicate the editor this way:

   Smith, Adam. "Frost's Crackle." *The Power of Poetry*. Ed.
      Susan Jones. New York: Simon, 1992.

In other words, if the abbreviation for *editor* follows a period,
it should be capitalized, just as the first word of a sentence is
capitalized. Otherwise, it is only an abbreviation for a common noun
and need not be capitalized.

Sometimes the smallest details require the most explanation. This is an example of a comment from the archive that can save an instructor a great deal of time while also providing the student with much more professional feedback. Explaining problems like this becomes almost impossible if you do not have the power of a computer and the archive.

Construct your Works Cited title correctly.

On the Works Cited page, the title of the Works Cited page should be exactly--not approximately--centered, one inch from the top of the page. It should not be underlined or italicized. It should not be in all-caps: WORKS CITED. It should not say Work Cited. It should only be double-spaced down from your name header, not triple or quadruple-spaced, and the works should be double-spaced down from the title. Do not use the outdated term *Bibliography* because we now list many works other than books. Please consult *Advanced Academic Writing* or the *MLA Handbook* for guidelines on such matters. The Works Cited title looks like this:

.........................top of page.........................

Smith 6

Works Cited

Adams, Susan. *New Developments in Poetic Form*. London: Oxford
    UP, 1975.
Johnson, John. *The Music of Beethoven*. New York: Scribner's,
    1993.

Here is another frequent location of errors. It seems impossible that students could make many mistakes just in the title of a Works Cited page, and yet, just as they do in the title of the paper at the front, students make many mistakes in the Works Cited title.

This is a good example of a comment that is perfect for this archive. As I gradually discovered more and more errors, I added variations to the comment until it was comprehensive. A student who would make one kind of title mistake often made a different kind of title mistake in the next paper, and so careful detail in the comment helped the students.

Notice that there are no blank lines between header and title or title and listings; it is all double-spaced.

Format the Works Cited page correctly.

Please study the proper construction of the Works Cited page. The basic order of a Works Cited listing is name of author or editor (these are in alphabetical order), period, two blank spaces, italicized title of book, period, two blank spaces, city, colon, blank space, abbreviated name of publisher, comma, blank space, date of publication, period. There are many variations, but this is the standard from which the variations vary. The basic form looks like this:

..........................top of page.........................

Smith 6

Works Cited

Adams, Susan. *New Developments in Poetic Form.* London: Oxford
     UP, 1975.

Johnson, John. *The Musical Life of Beethoven.* New York:
     Scribner's, 1993.

---. *The Whimsical Life of Mozart.* New York: Harcourt, 1991.

Smith, Rebecca and James McMichael. *Metaphor: Meaning and
     Intention.* Chicago: U of Chicago P, 1984.

Notice that the title of each work is in italics, not placed in upper case or quotation marks. We used to underline the title of a book, but the new MLA rules call for italics instead. Notice that we give only city, not state. When more than one city is listed in the book, use only the major American city, which will usually be New York. Works Cited must be placed in alphabetical order by authors' last names; they are not numbered. When an author is used twice, the name is replaced the second time by a triple hyphen and a period. The listings are double-spaced, and the second line--not the first--of each listing is indented five spaces. There must be a period at the end of every listing, and two blank spaces after each period inside the listing. Do not use N.Y. as a city designation; write the words out: New York. Remember that the same one-inch margins, left and right, apply to the Works Cited as to the rest of the paper. Page numbers are usually not necessary at the end of a Works Cited listing because you give the page numbers in your documentary notes.

MLA

When you list two books by the same author in your Works Cited, do not repeat the author's name twice. In the second listing, replace the author's name with a triple hyphen followed by a period: ---. Be sure to use hyphens (---.) rather than underlines (___.). See *Advanced Academic Writing* for examples.

You use the triple hyphen only on the Works Cited page, not in a corresponding parenthetical note. Instead of (--- 94) use the author's name and a clue word from the book title: (Shakespeare Shrew 94).

The sheer length and detail of this two-page comment is an indication of its importance and of the many elements that must be mastered before the page is perfect. The Works Cited page has so many dimensions that students sometimes have many mistakes on the page. It is not unusual for first-time students to have several mistakes in each listing.

Students must devote intense attention to the Works Cited page, which means that we must impress the importance upon them in the initial instruction. The listings have an importance beyond the student's paper because other people's work is involved, and it is a serious thing to list a title or name incorrectly, or to present a citation with shabby punctuation or errors. If anything should be perfect, it is the Works Cited page, and we want students to feel that responsibility.

Abbreviate publishers' names.

Abbreviate publishers' names in the Works Cited listings. In
your Works Cited page, you fail to follow the MLA instructions
for abbreviating the names of publishing houses. Avoid including
unnecessary words such as *Publishing*, *Company*, and *Inc*. Condense
long names such as *Harcourt, Brace, Jovanovitch* down into the short
ones listed in the *MLA Handbook*: Harcourt. Instead of *Charles
Scribner's Sons* it is only *Scribner's* (do not forget the apostrophe
in that one). *Prentice-Hall* is just *Prentice*. Do not write out
the words *University* or *Press*: instead of *Indiana University Press*
it is simply *Indiana UP*; instead of *University of Michigan Press*
it is simply *U of Michigan P*. Notice that you do not put a period
after the *U* or the *P*. See the *MLA Handbook* for the complete list
of correct abbreviations, and if a company is not listed there,
just apply these principles of succinctness intelligently when you
encounter an unlisted firm. Study the abbreviations below:

...........................top of page.........................

Smith 6

Works Cited

Adams, Susan. *New Developments in Poetic Form*. London: Oxford
    UP, 1975.

Johnson, John. *The Musical Life of Beethoven*. New York:
    Scribner's, 1993.

---. *The Whimsical Life of Mozart*. New York: Harcourt, 1991.

Smith, Rebecca and James McMichael. *Metaphor: Meaning and
    Intention*. Chicago: U of Chicago P, 1984.

The abbreviation of publishers' names is another example of the MLA method's
elegant way of reducing the format to what counts, of eliminating unnecessary
details or distractions.

Use *et al* for multiple authors.

When there are three or more authors or editors of a work you are citing, you do not have to list out all of their names in the Works Cited listing if you do not wish to. Instead, you may list only the first author, put a comma, and type the Latin term *et al* which is short for *et alia*, and others. You do not need to put et al in italics in the Works Cited.

...........................top of page..........................

Smith 6

Works Cited

Adams, Susan. *New Developments in Poetic Form*. London: Oxford UP, 1975.

Darden, Susan, **et al**. *The Elements of Composition*. New York: Scribner's, 2001.

Johnson, John. *The Whimsical Life of Mozart*. New York: Harcourt, 1991.

Smith, Rebecca and James McMichael. *Metaphor: Meaning and Intention*. Chicago: U of Chicago P, 1984.

Because many small standards can affect the listings in a Works Cited page, I needed many comments about those small details. This is another example of a comment that is perfect for the archive: it requires detail to explain, it is a problem encountered often, and it is a concrete standard that does not need a customized comment to fit the student's particular error.

```
Avoid widows and orphans.
Please avoid widows and orphans.  Note that you should avoid widows
(a single line at the bottom of the page that belongs with a
paragraph or quotation on the following page) and orphans (a single
line at the top of a page that belongs with a paragraph or quotation
on the previous page), even though adjusting the paper may result in
a top or bottom margin that is wider or shorter than the one-inch
standard.
     Avoid orphan parentheticals, too.  Sometimes a parenthetical
note from the bottom of a long quotation becomes an orphan when the
quote ends on the bottom line of one page and the note appears on the
top line of the next page; when this happens, you must go back and
make adjustments so the parenthetical will fit on the previous page
with its quote; the parenthetical should not be left as an orphan.
```

The point here is to avoid a single line of a paragraph or long quotation appearing at either the top or the bottom of a page. You want to keep at least two lines of a paragraph or long quotation together. If possible, keep a long quotation together entirely, and under no circumstances should you let the quotation appear on one page and its parenthetical on the next page. This sometimes requires some rewording to make things fit better. We do not want the top of the page or the bottom of the page to sever blocks of thought.

Use Courier type font, not Helvetica or Times Roman.
In an academic research paper, it is better to use the Courier type
font--which is what I am using in these comments--rather than Helvetica
which is a sans-serif modern font that looks like this--or Times Roman--which is a traditional
font used in newspapers and books and that looks like this--for several reasons.
Courier is exceptionally open and readable, especially when double-
spaced. Courier may be specified by colleges and universities for
research papers and for theses in advanced degrees.

    Note that for purposes of precise indenting, the Courier type
font (you are looking at Courier now) is superior; it is a monofont
in which each letter takes up the same width, whereas in a variable-width font
such as Times Roman that I am typing in now, each letter is a different width, and
it is impossible to tell if you have indented properly. That is why
I require you to type your papers not in Times but in Courier.

Sometimes someone will protest the choice of Courier, preferring the appearance of, say, Times Roman. He or she may also protest the ragged-right policy, preferring the appearance of a justified page. I understand the point, and as you see, when I am writing a paragraph for a book, such as this paragraph, I myself choose Times, justified. A research paper, however, is a different matter. We are teaching students to follow standards, and one of the most important standards is spacing. Putting two spaces where one is the standard is just like putting two *o*'s in the word *open*. A space is a language object, just as a letter is, and spacing can be incorrect. There are rules for spaces between words, spaces after sentences, spaces before paragraphs, spaces for long quotations, spaces for second lines in Works Cited—all of these must be checked for correctness. For teaching academic writing, a variable width font and justified page will not do.

93

Marcus,

Thank you for this outstanding paper on Thomas Jefferson's crucial role in establishing the shape of the American democratic philosophy. Like everyone else, I had read books and articles about Jefferson, but I had never thought as deeply as you did about how his specific language stamped the way all of us think about our rights as citizens. Anyone who read your paper would be impressed with how solidly you make a research-based case for your thesis, that it was Jefferson who wrote the words in our minds. Of course, there are always a few problems that need to be improved next time, so let us look at a few of those; I will give page numbers with some comments to help you find the problem in your paper.

Page 1.
Do not put an apostrophe before the *s* in a date. (1800s)
In punctuating centuries, such as the 1800s or the 1900s, do not insert an apostrophe before the *s*. For example, you should type 1700s rather than 1700's. This is correct: "During the 1970s Borges returned to writing fiction."

Page 2.
Avoid using *this* as the subject of the verb. (ref)
Please avoid using the demonstrative pronoun *this* as the subject of a sentence. Use it as an adjective, referring to this idea, this policy, this poem. When you just say "this altered everything," there is almost always ambiguity, leaving the reader to wonder precisely what *this* is referring to.

Page 2.
You have used the wrong word. (w)
Choose your words carefully. My mark *w* means that you have used the wrong word. It is easy to use a word that sounds impressive but that has a wrong or even absurd meaning in your sentence. If, for example, you say that "Sinclair's family sided with the movements of the Confederacy,"

Comments about Punctuation

```
Your clause punctuation is excellent.
Please do not misuse commas.
Do not put an apostrophe before the s in a date.   (1800s)
Learn to use possessive apostrophes correctly.
Use brackets [] to insert within quotes.
Use the list colon correctly.
Learn how to use a colon before a long quotation.
Use a colon between title and subtitle.
Put a comma after some long introductory elements.
Put a comma after multiple introductory prepositional phrases.
Avoid run-on sentences.   (R-O)
Appositives should be enclosed in commas.
Remember appositive commas for year, city, and nation.
Punctuate D,I complex sentences correctly.
Do not put a comma in an ID complex sentence.
Avoid comma splices.
Do not forget the list comma.
Use a semicolon in an I;I compound sentence.   (I;I)
Construct dashes and hyphens correctly.
Learn how to use and construct the ellipsis.   ( . . . )
Minimize your use of hyphens.
Use italics for things-as-such.
Place titles in italics.
Put no comma in a parenthetical.
Punctuate parenthetical documentary notes correctly.
Punctuate quotation marks correctly.
Learn how to punctuate quotations within quotations.
Use a semicolon before however.
Study the difference between semicolons and colons.
You may use a slash (/) in poem quotes.
Follow the rules for blank spaces.   (#)
Space correctly in documentation.
Type two blank spaces after closing punctuation marks.
Use continuous underlining.
Do not underline inappropriate punctuation.
```

Academic punctuation is a function of grammar and can only be learned after all four levels of grammar have been learned. That is the fast, efficient, clear way to approach punctuation. It is impossible to put a comma after an introductory participial phrase intentionally if you do not know the phrase when you see it. Without grammar knowledge, how can you avoid putting a comma after a gerund phrase used as the subject of the verb?

```
Your clause punctuation is excellent.
You have done a good job punctuating the clauses in your sentences.
I do not see any run-on sentences or comma splices in the paper.
Attention to details like that makes a big difference in how pleasant
a paper is for a reader to read.
```

Here is an important but quick comment that shows the student we notice and appreciate an important writing achievement. Because every sentence—EVERY sentence—has one clause or more, every sentence has a clause punctuation decision to make. If a student has written a paper of 450 sentences, then 450 clause decisions had to be made. When there are zero clause punctuation errors, that is a noteworthy accomplishment, and it is more than worth a quick copy and paste to congratulate the student.

The general rule for clause punctuation in compound sentences and complex sentences, at least at the introductory level, is:

COMPOUND: I;I   I,ccI
COMPLEX: D,I   ID

where *I* stands for independent clause, *D* stands for dependent clause, and *cc* stands for coordinating conjunction. See *The Magic Lens* or *Grammar Voyage* for more detail.

```
Please do not misuse commas.
Use commas correctly.  While we do use commas to separate clauses
in compound sentences and to separate introductory phrases or
dependent clauses, we do not use commas to separate compound parts
of a sentence such as compound subjects, compound verbs, or compound
direct objects.  We also do not use a comma to separate subject from
verb; these belong together, not apart.  If you type "Livvie and
Cash, went back to the house" you are separating the subject from
the verb with a comma.  Please review the uses of the comma.
```

Sometimes a student will only make one or two kinds of comma punctuation error, but sometimes a student will make many kinds of punctuation errors, and he or she needs to review comma punctuation entirely. That is the purpose of this comment.

A general proclivity is for students to overuse commas, attempting to put them at places they think sound good, places where they think they hear a pause in expression—but you cannot hear commas. That is not how academic punctuation operates, and students who do not know both their grammar and their comma rules will make comma errors.

In principle we want as few commas as necessary in the sentence. We need commas to keep pieces of grammar—which means pieces of logic—separate.

```
Do not put an apostrophe before the s in a date.  (1800s)
In punctuating centuries, such as the 1800s or the 1900s, do not
insert an apostrophe before the s.  For example, you should type
1700s rather than 1700's.  This is correct: "During the 1970s Borges
returned to writing fiction."
```

Here is a detail that is easy for students to master if they focus on it. It is one of those details that you can learn if you stare it down once. The MLA method regards the year apostrophe as superfluous. It is another small reason that the MLA style is so clean and readable.

This is an academic aesthetic. In the MLA style all of the concern is for the reader's experience. The method results in a paper that is smooth-looking, easy on the eyes, uncluttered, free of pointless academic frippery. Much of the visual clutter of a traditional research paper has been removed, leaving the truth of the argument in the clear, with the Spartan minimum of its documentation.

Learn to use possessive apostrophes correctly.
We always make a noun, singular or plural, possessive by ADDING
something to it. We make singular nouns possessive by adding
an apostrophe and an *s*, even when the noun already ends in *s*.
Thus, we would type poetess's, not poetess'; Euripides's, not
Euripides'; Dickens's, not Dickens'; Herodotus's, not Herodotus';
and Sophocles's, not Sophocles'. If the noun is plural instead of
singular, then we simply add the apostrophe: the dogs' houses, many
authors' ideas.

In no case would we take a plural noun such as *authors* or a
proper noun such as *Socrates* and insert an apostrophe into it because
it ends in *s*: Socrate's! His name was not *Socrate*. Apostrophes
never mutilate words. We form possessives only by ADDING either an
apostrophe or an apostrophe and an *s*. The possessive of the proper
noun *Parmenides* is *Parmenides's*, not *Parmenide's*; the sophist's name
was not *Parmenide*!

Caution: Do not use apostrophes in ordinary plurals that are not
possessive: "Epictetus taught that ordinary philosopher's were free"
is an error because no apostrophe should be used; the word should be
an ordinary plural common noun: *philosophers*.

Some style manuals would let you drop the *s* after singular
possessives, but I would prefer that you do not; I prefer the old-
fashioned way, Dickens's, which is also preferred by MLA and by Strunk
and White in their classic text, *The Elements of Style*.

Apostrophe errors are among the most common and intractable student errors.
The explanation must be complete and clear. It would be almost impossible
to handwrite or even type an explanation this long every time you see an
apostrophe error, which is in almost every paper, but with the archive you can
quickly copy and paste.

```
Use brackets [] to insert within quotes.
Use brackets [like this] for inserting words into quotations.
When you insert words into quotations--usually for the purpose of
clarifying references or enhancing the flow of the sentences--you
must enclose your inserted words in brackets like [this] to show the
reader that these words were not part of the original quote.  Be
sure to use [brackets] rather than (parentheses) or <mathematical
symbols>.  Do not put spaces inside the brackets; it should look
[like this] and not [ like this ].
```

This comment reiterates a standard addressed before, but here it is more focused on the pure punctuation of brackets, giving me an option that I sometimes needed.

The issue here is the sanctity of quotations. When we say we are quoting someone, it must be true—absolutely true. We cannot add a word or omit a word or change a tense or do anything else that alters the other person's words in any way, unless we follow strict rules for such changes.

The change featured here is the insertion of a word or words into a quotation. By convention scholars know that when they see brackets in a quotation, the brackets signify that the words inside the brackets were added for clarity and were not part of the original quotation. When we take words out of a quotation, we indicate that with an ellipsis (. . .) where the missing words used to be; that will be explained on page 125.

Use the list colon correctly.

You misunderstand the use of the colon (:) before a list. We do not use the colon when the list of items is really a compound direct object: "Stephen Crane wrote poetry, short stories, and novels." We also do not use the colon when the list is a compound subject complement: "Crane was a reporter, a poet, and a novelist." Finally, we do not need a colon if there is a nice connecting word such as *including* or *as*: "Crane wrote many novels, including *The Red Badge of Courage*, *Maggie*, and *George's Mother*."

So when do we use a colon to introduce a list? We use a colon when a list is only a list, tacked on to provide examples: "Crane wrote many kinds of works: poems, stories, and novels." We also use the list colon after the phrase "the following," as in this case: "Crane wrote the following: *Maggie*, *George's Mother*, and *The Red Badge of Courage*." Notice in these two cases that the list is not connected to the sentence by grammar; it is added on. That is why the colon is needed--because the list is, in a way, outside the sentence structure.

Other correct locations for a colon are to introduce a long quotation and between a title and subtitle.

I used to be surprised to see students inserting colons after verbs leading to compound direct objects. After years of correcting that error, I was no longer surprised. The solution is for the students to understand the grammar better. We do not use colons before direct objects, not even if they are double, triple, or quadruple compound. This is another great example of a comment that is really only possible if you have an archive; with an archive, it is easy to provide such an elaborate explanation.

Learn how to use a colon before a long quotation.
Introduce long quotations with a colon. When you write a sentence
to introduce a long quotation (or short in some cases), and the long
quotation is the evidence or example to which you refer, it is best
to conclude your introductory sentence with a colon (:) rather than
a period. (Also, do not use a semicolon.) This lets the reader be
certain of the status of the quotation--as an illustration of what
you have just said. A colon is also better than no punctuation at
all if the quotation serves to complete the thought begun by your
introductory sentence; you might, for instance, introduce a quotation
with a sentence such as:

In his commentary Marcus Fenix explains that Salinger is:

> . . . an example of how the modern novel turned inwards.
> Holden Caulfield is a classic case of introspection
> run amok. Holden second-guesses everything he does,
> undercutting his every decision with agonizing doubts about
> how it will be perceived. (Fenix 162)

The colon before the long quotation is one of the details that many students learn late, but it is a graceful way of flowing into a quotation, maintaining the train of thought. The colon in this case has a feeling to it, a logical aesthetic, that makes the nature of the quotation as an illustration clear.

Use a colon between title and subtitle.

When you have a subtitle to the main title of your paper, use a colon between the title and subtitle. If both the title and subtitle are short and fit easily on one line, then you can do that, but if they do not fit, then put the entire subtitle on a second line by itself, below the title. The colon should also be used between title and subtitle in the Works Cited listing. Do NOT insert a blank space before the colon : like that. The colon should immediately follow the title, and then be followed by a single blank space, like this:

Ernest Hemingway: His Farewell to Arms.

Ernest Hemingway:
A Writer Paralyzed by the Fear of Adjectives

Here is another concrete comment about a punctuation detail. What I found was that as a class, students would misuse the colon in every imaginable way, and that students who made one colon mistake in one paper would make a different colon mistake in the next paper. The best plan was to explain all of the variations.

Put a comma after some long introductory elements.
We usually use a comma after a long introductory element to a sentence. For example, we use a comma after an introductory participial phrase, after an introductory dependent clause, after a long introductory prepositional phrase, and after multiple introductory prepositional phrases. The comma lets the reader know when the introductory element has ended. What is long? Well, I usually use a comma if the introductory elements is five words or more, but there can be no absolute rule here; it is a matter of judgment. If a two- or three-word introductory element creates confusion because it lacks a subsequent comma, then use one. Examples of correct commas are:
    From the earliest and fiercest days, we continued to hope.
    At the beginning of the century, a new era dawned.
    Devouring the unlucky prey, the lion growled.
    When the bough breaks, the cradle will fall.

This comma indicates a particular spot in the logic of a sentence; it lets the reader know that the introductory section is complete, often clarifying what is modifying and what is modified. We want students to understand the different variations but also to understand what the variations have in common, as introductory elements.

Put a comma after multiple introductory prepositional phrases.
Put a comma after multiple introductory prepositional phrases but not
after a single short introductory prepositional phrase. You may use
a comma after a long introductory prepositional phrase, generally
five words or more. You may also use a comma if a short introductory
phrase without a comma results in a confusion of meaning.

This is a more specific comment that focuses on the use of the comma with
introductory prepositional phrases. Sometimes you need a more complete
comment, and sometimes you need a more specific comment.

Avoid run-on sentences.   (R-O)

My mark R-O means that you have written a run-on sentence. It is called a run-on sentence because it runs on from clause to clause without pausing between clauses in order to give the two independent ideas their just separation. A run-on sentence happens when you fail to put the comma in an I,ccI compound sentence, or you fail to put the semicolon in an I;I compound sentence. Two independent clauses joined by a coordinating conjunction (*and, but, or, nor, for, so, yet*) must have a comma before the coordinating conjunction: "Melville wrote to Hawthorne, and Hawthorne wrote back." If there is no coordinating conjunction between the clauses, then you use a semicolon to separate them: "Melville wrote to Hawthorne; Hawthorne wrote back." You have to make a decision about clause punctuation every time you write a sentence.

The run-on sentence is one side of the clause punctuation principle. It is best taught in that context as part of a complete presentation of the punctuation of compound and complex sentences. This description makes use of the abbreviated mnemonic I use to teach clause punctuation in *The Magic Lens* and other texts; in this model, *I* stands for independent clause, *D* stands for dependent clause, and *cc* stands for coordinating conjunction:

I,ccI

I;I

D, I

ID

Appositives should be enclosed in commas.

It is good to use appositives--interrupting definitions--to insert information gracefully into sentences, especially early in a research paper when you might be mentioning names or titles unfamiliar to the reader, but remember that appositives take TWO COMMAS or none-- usually two, and you must not forget the second appositive comma: Ted Hughes, Plath's former husband, wrote in praise of Plath's writings. Charles VIII, King of France, invaded and conquered Italy.

     If you forget the second comma, you can have a catastrophe: Pauling, a Nobel Prize winner wishes to speak with you. Here the missing comma changes the sentence such that we are now speaking to Pauling instead of about him, and telling him that someone else wishes to speak with him, instead of saying that Pauling wishes to speak with you. The missing comma destroys the logic of the sentence.

     If the appositive phrase comes at the end of the sentence, then obviously the second comma is replaced by a period: We went to see Linus Pauling, the Nobel Prize winner.

     Another exception to this rule is the one-word appositive, such as: "My old friend Bob arrived early." In this case the appositive *Bob* does not require commmas.

It is essential for students to master appositive punctuation because appositives are such an important component in academic writing. An appositive phrase is a much more graceful way of explaining who or what you are talking about than waiting until the next sentence to clear it up; waiting leaves the reader in the dark needlessly.

Remember appositive commas for year, city, and nation.
Please remember that the year, city, and nation are often used as
appositives and therefore require commas before and after. Thus,
we say "August 20, 1947, was hot" or "Dublin, Ireland, is damp" or
"Chicago, Illinois, is busy" and we are required to put the second
comma in each case.

   Failure to put the second comma usually warps the meaning of the
sentence, because it makes the second word, rather than the first,
the subject of a verb. What if someone asks where I am going, and
I answer, "Chicago, Illinois is my home." That means I am going
to Chicago, but my home is somewhere in Illinois. If I answer,
"Chicago, Illinois, is my home," then I mean Chicago is my home. To
change commas is to change meanings. Put a comma before and after an
appositive.

Even though we do not always need to enclose one-word appositives in commas,
here are three cases where we do. Having this comment stored in the archive
for a quick cut and paste is useful.

Punctuate D,I complex sentences correctly.

My mark D,I means that you have forgotten to put a comma after the introductory dependent clause in a D,I complex sentence. A complex sentence contains an independent clause and a dependent clause. If the complex sentence is in ID order, then we generally do not put a comma between clauses, but when the sentence is in DI order, then we put a comma after the introductory dependent clause. For example, we would use a comma to separate the D,I structure, "When Goethe was a young author, he wrote *The Sorrows of Young Werther*," but we would not use one if the structure were reversed to ID: "Goethe wrote *The Sorrows of Young Werther* when he was a young author."

One common form of D,I sentence that seems to give trouble is the if/then sentence. Known in computer science as Boolean logic, the if/then structure is actually a D,I complex structure in grammar. The IF clause is dependent, and the THEN clause is regarded as independent, even though it begins with then. So we would punctuate the sentence, "If the country evolved into authoritarianism, then the people would lose their freedoms." The logic is this:

D , I

If A , then B.

By the way, the D,I comma is one beginner's rule that is sometimes broken in professional writing, but it is best to learn to do it this way. The D,I comma will never be regarded as incorrect, but its absence will usually be regarded as an error.

Good clause punctuation provides clarity to ideas and is a standard expected in all academic writing. Clause punctuation is only possible after the acquisition of clause vision, which is established in level four of the four-level analysis. Students who do not know grammar cannot learn clause punctuation.

Do not put a comma in an ID complex sentence. (ID)
Remember not to use a comma in an ID complex sentence such as
"Socrates would not teach because he said he had nothing to teach."
If the independent clause comes first, no comma: ID. If the dependent
clause comes first, then put a comma: D,I. "Because he had nothing
to teach, Socrates would not teach." I expect you to follow the
clause punctuation rules we have studied: (I;I I,ccI D,I ID).
Every time you write a sentence you must make a conscious clause
punctuation decision.

Students may not realize the magnitude of the fact that every sentence, EVERY sentence, has one or more clauses. This means that clause punctuation is an issue in every sentence they write. This standard is relentless and will never go away, so students must master it.

Avoid comma splices.

The comma splice (I,I) is a form of clause punctuation error. It happens when you try to connect two independent clauses with a mere comma instead of with a strong semicolon. An example of a comma splice would be, "Melville worked on the island, Melville enjoyed island life." Another would be, "The first set of Plato's *Dialogues* gave a general sense of Socrates, his feelings, thoughts, and ideas were all expressed in these dialogues." Remember, you make a compound sentence by joining two independent clauses either with a comma and a coordinating conjunction, or with a semicolon if there is no conjunction. You cannot splice two independent clauses together with a comma alone; the comma is not a strong connection; it is only a minor pause. In other words the rule is I;I and not I,I.

Once again clause punctuation emerges as a source of error. What happens as we become more aware of the technical aspects of academic writing is that forms become visible; we suddenly know we are moving a participial phrase from one place in a sentence to another place in the sentence, or we suddenly know that we have two independent clauses that are making a double-thought. With two independent clauses, we cannot put them together with the comma; we must use a semicolon or the comma-coordinating-conjunction. The comma blurs the two forms; it is messy because the separate identity of the two forms is no longer clear.

```
Use a semicolon in an I;I compound sentence.  (I;I)
Use a semicolon to separate the independent clauses of an I;I
compound sentence.  You must use a semicolon to separate the two
clauses in a compound sentence that does not contain a coordinating
conjunction to join the two clauses.  The structure is I;I.
Example: "Dido is an important character in Virgil's poem; she
speaks 188 of the 700 lines in Book Four."

      This semicolon technique is especially effective when you are
using a compound sentence in order to unify a parallel:  "Some of
these characters were lovely; some were hideous."
```

Here is the reverse view of the comma splice comment, which showed what not to do with this structure. We want to emphasize the logic of the structure, not just the authority of the rule; semicolons signify a bond of meaning between what is to their left and right. If that connection of meaning and logic is not there, then it is not defensible to present the idea as a compound sentence because two simple sentences would be more true. Like everything else in writing, punctuation is expected to be the truth. A punctuation mark that indicates something contrary to fact is not just wrong; it is false.

Do not forget the list comma.

Remember the list comma before the coordinating conjunction. When you are listing items of three or more, please use a comma between all items, including before the coordinating conjunction that precedes the final item. Say that life is "nasty, brutish, and short," not that it is "nasty, brutish and short."

Some manuals would allow you to drop that final comma, but I would prefer that you retain it. If you do not retain the list comma, then you lose the ability to distinguish between saying the woods are "lovely, dark and deep" and saying the woods are "lovely, dark, and deep." The first version means that the dark depth is lovely, but the second version means that the woods are three things.

Commas change meanings. Notice that two items do not make a list; they make a compound, which does not require a comma.

This is a small detail that matters. In the case of the Robert Frost quotation above, the line was originally punctuated with the final comma after an editor inserted the comma before the conjunction. The punctuation was later restored to Frost's original design; scholars realized that Frost was not saying that the woods were three things; he was saying that dark depth was lovely. That is the difference between:

The woods are lovely, dark, and deep.

The woods are lovely, dark and deep.

Construct dashes and hyphens correctly.
Please notice exactly the difference between the way dashes and hyphens are made. In Times Roman font a true dash is simply a longer mark than a hyphen (it looks like this—not this-see?), but in Courier type font, a dash is a two-hyphen mark of punctuation used to indicate abrupt breaks in thought--like that, whereas a hyphen is a one-stroke mark used to join words into one-thought units.

   Some manuals suggest that you make a dash with two blank spaces and only one hyphen - like that, but I prefer that you do not. I prefer two hyphens and no spaces for a dash, and one hyphen and no spaces for a hyphen, and then there is no doubt which mark you really intended--see?

Here is another tiny detail that makes an enormous difference. Not only might students not notice the difference between dashes and hyphens when they see them in books, but the two signs, — and -, have opposite logical meanings. The dash separates thoughts—but the hyphen joins two words together into single-word structures.

To make the situation more complicated for beginners, the dash is constructed very differently in Courier from the way it appears in a book. A student who sees—this in a book must type--this in a paper.

Learn how to use and construct the ellipsis. (. . .)
We use an ellipsis, a series of spaces and periods, to indicate
that we have left out part of a quotation. If you are only quoting
a phrase, you need no ellipsis at all: We saw by the "dawn's early
light." We need not begin a short quote with an ellipsis if a lower-
case letter clearly indicates that the first word quoted was not the
first word of the sentence: Fitzgerald replied that he "needed no
instructions from Hemingway." We do begin a long quote with a three-
period ellipsis if we have left out the beginning of the sentence.
A simple omission within a sentence requires a three-period ellipsis
with spaces before and after every period: "But as for me . . . give
me death." If you are omitting the end of a question, you put the
question mark after the ellipsis: We would ask "How many angels can
dance . . . ?" Finally, if we are omitting the final word or words
of a sentence (or more than one sentence), we must include a fourth
period--the one to end the sentence: "Mary had a little lamb. . . .
And everywhere that Mary went the lamb was sure to go." Notice the
spacing; the extra period occurs immediately after the final quoted
word, with no intervening space. If you are using documentary notes
(as we do in our research papers) and you stop quoting right after
the ellipsis, then you put the extra period AFTER the documentary
note: As Mother Goose has noted, "Mary had a little lamb. Its
fleece was white . . ." (Goose 472).

Yes, the use of the ellipsis is complicated, and so the ellipsis instructions are
another example of the power of the archive; without an archive, you simply
could not provide this kind of feedback to every student who makes an ellipsis
error.

```
Miminize your use of hyphens.
Do not overuse hyphens at the ends of the lines.  It is best to avoid
breaking words with hyphens, unless you break a very long word in its
middle.  Otherwise, do not hyphenate in a way that leaves only one to
three letters of a word at the end of the line.  It is better for the
right margin to be a bit more ragged than for the reader to find short
syllables of words at the ends of the lines.  These short, incomplete
syllables are a slight interruption to the smooth flow of thought.
The hyphen breaks the word in two jagged pieces.
```

The idea here is an aesthetic one, a question of unities versus fragments. If you look back through this book, you will see that I disable the automatic hyphenation feature; if I did not, the computer would leave chunks of broken words everywhere, three or four per page. I want the eye to see the whole word in one place, not half of the word to the right and the other half of the word to the left.

I even feel that way about phrases and clauses; when I make a slide to show at a conference or workshop, I avoid ending a line in the middle of a prepositional phrase, or ending a line with an adjective if its noun will be on the next line. I want the adjective and its noun to be side by side. I want to keep grammatical groups together because they are logical units—mind units. I want the eye to take in the entire phrase without having first to look here and then to look there.

This is the same sensibility that makes us prefer to write the subject and verb side by side, avoiding intervening phrases or adjective clauses if possible. I even try to preserve the visual capture of a paragraph, so I will edit a page so that the reader does not have to turn the page to see the end of a paragraph. The more unities a paper has, the clearer it is. When we move thoughts from our minds to a page, we want to avoid breakage.

Use *italics* for things-as-such.

Please remember that words, numbers, and letters as such must be placed in *italics*. In the past we used <u>underlining</u> to indicate italics, but today the MLA method requires *true italics*. In this way we distinguish the word *dog* from the animal, dog. We use *b*'s in spelling, and we use *3*'s in counting. See?

We also place foreign language words in italics: Homer begins his story *in medias res*, in the middle of things. This technique will be especially important when you are analyzing poetry or literature and are making reference to the words, letters, or sounds contained in the writing. Be sure to avoid the common mistake of putting words as such in quotation marks; we do not refer to the word "shibboleth" but to the word *shibboleth*.

This comment represents a change from the traditional use of underlining. In the past we used typewriters that could not create actual italics, and so we indicated italics by underlining. Even after computer word processors became available, we continued to use underlining in Courier type font because underlining seemed to be clearer and better looking in Courier. The Modern Language Association, however, has now changed the standard, requiring true italics where underlining was previously used. Part of the message we want to give to students is that we adhere to the MLA standard, without making exceptions for personal preferences, so we will now use italics for the items listed above and for titles.

Place titles in italics.

Please remember that the titles of books, newspapers, ships, trains, works of art, major musical compositions, and other important titles are always to be placed in italics, both in the body of your paper and in your Works Cited. In other words, when you see a title in a book, the title might look like this: A Midsummer Night's Dream, but in a research paper it will look like this: *A Midsummer Night's Dream*. It does not matter that the title of the book was not in italics on the cover of the book.

Titles should not be placed in quotation marks or in upper case in lieu of italics. Less significant titles, such as the titles of chapters, articles, poems, or songs, do not deserve italics; these minor titles are only placed in quotation marks. In a Works Cited listing, book titles are to be italicized; they are not also enclosed in quotation marks. A Works Cited listing, therefore, will look like this:

Thompson, Michael Clay. *Opus 40*. Unionville: Royal Fireworks, 2010.

This comment focuses on a different detail but continues the instruction for using italics. I used to be surprised that after all of my patient explanations, students would still forget to put the book titles in the Works Cited page in italics. I eventually realized that a research paper is a complicated assignment; you cannot learn it in one pass. Most students have so many details to master that they can only master one layer of them per paper. After enough papers, students finally master it.

```
Put no comma in a parenthetical.
Do not use commas in the parenthetical documentary notes.  In a
parenthetical documentary notation, no comma is used between the
author's name and the page number.  The note should look like this
(Euripides 64), not like this (Euripides, 64).
```

Here is a punctuation standard required by the MLA method. It is another example of the modern, minimal aesthetic of MLA. I appreciate the MLA standards because I have a strong sense that good writing means clearing away the noise and debris so that the ideas can stand out. A comma in a parenthetical contributes no clarity but create a little smudge.

This comment is a focused one that I could use when this comma error seemed to be a special concern in a student's paper. If I needed more elaborate instruction for parentheticals, I could use the following comment.

Punctuate parenthetical documentary notes correctly.
It is important to punctuate correctly when you are using
parenthetical documentary notes. In short quotations the period
comes after the parenthetical note, rather than at the end of the
sentence, "like this" (Thompson 56). If your short quotation
concludes with a question mark or exclamation point, you still put
a period after the parenthetical note, "like this!" (Thompson 56).
You do NOT put a period both inside the quotation marks and after
the parenthetical note: "this is incorrect." (Thompson 56).

> In long quotations that are indented ten spaces, the
> period comes at the end of the sentence and before the
> parenthetical note, like this. (Thompson 56)

Notice that there are two blank spaces after the period, there is
no comma inside the note, between the name and the page number, and
there is no period inside the note after the page number.

If you are not quoting, but are only paraphrasing or using
a parenthetical note to document an idea that you have found in
research, then the period should follow the parenthetical at the end
of the sentence, like this (Thompson 56).

This comment grew, weed-like, for years. It is another illustration of how many different ways students miss the mark on what seems to be a small and obvious requirement. One point that emerges from this is that many students are beginners, barely beginning beginners, and it is easy to underestimate the swarm of details that they have never seen. With the archive we can easily paste in a detailed explanation like this.

Punctuate quotation marks correctly.

Put commas and periods INSIDE quotation marks. When you are
combining quotation marks with other punctuation, it is important
to place the marks of punctuation in the proper order. Periods and
commas go inside quotation marks, "like this," rather than outside
"like this", and semicolons and colons go outside quotation marks,
"like this"; question marks and exclamation points go either inside
or outside, depending upon whether they are part of the quotation or
not: "This is an example!" Notice that parenthetical notes create
exceptions to these rules, since in a short quotation, we put the
comma after the note instead of inside the quotation marks, "like
this" (Jones 76).

Because a research paper is the occasion for many quotation marks, the rules
for quotation marks ascend to a status they do not normally achieve. Students
will be using quotation marks constantly and will therefore have to know the
standards for combining quotation marks with other marks of punctuation.

Learn to punctuate quotations within quotations.
Sometimes a quotation will have a smaller quotation inside it, and
this requires its own standard to avoid confusion. If you have
to present quotes within short quotes, use apostrophes as single
quotation marks for the innermost quotation: According to Smith,
"Jones once said 'Bark like a dog.'" Do it like that. For quotes
within quotes within quotes within quotes, keep alternating between
single and double quotation marks.

    For quotes within indented long quotations, the long quotation
has no quotation marks around it, so you may place the interior
quote in doubles, then go to singles if there is a third quotation
inside the second quotation.

This situation does not happen often, but it does happen, Imagine the mess
that would occur if we used the same kinds of quotation marks in all cases;
a reader would have no idea which quote was ending where. The simple
expedient of using singles inside of doubles and going back to doubles if there
is a quote inside of that one helps us keep everything tidy.

Use a semicolon before *however*.

When you use an adverb such as *however* or *therefore* to begin the second clause of a sentence, use a semicolon before it and a comma afterwards: "Melville developed a realistic style; however, it contained overtones of philosophical importance," or, "The author seems sympathetic; however, he is only being ironic."

This is a detail that students might not catch on their first paper. The instruction will take more solidly if we emphasize the grammatical structure involved.

```
Study the difference between semicolons and colons.
Use a semicolon in a I;I compound sentence if there is no
coordinating conjunction to separate the two independent clauses; a
mere comma in this situation would be a comma splice error.  Use a
colon instead of a semicolon if the second clause is offered as an
illustration or example of what you said in the first clause: this
clause is such an example.  You should also study the way semicolons
can be used in lists, and the way colons can be used to introduce
lists.
```

You see that I needed a collection of comments about clauses and their punctuation to account for the ways the problems popped up in student papers. I would use this one when the accumulation of errors in a paper indicated that a student was confusing semicolons and colons.

You may use a slash (/) in poem quotes.
When you are quoting poetry in your research paper, you do not have to return to a new line just because you reach the end of a line of the poem. Instead of returning to a new line, you may just insert a slash (/) at the point where the poem drops to a new line. Do not use spaces before and after the slash: Mary had a little lamb,/Its fleece was white as snow,/And every where that Mary went/The lamb was sure to go. The slash will separate the lines of poetry for the reader. Of course, you can quote the lines in a column as they appear in the book if you prefer.

Here is a nice detail, a sort of elite detail, that feels scholarly.

There are many times, especially when we are quoting only a couple of lines of a poem, that we do not want to break our paragraph; we simply want to include the poem quote as a part of our paragraph, and this slash technique gives us a way to do that.

Follow the rules for blank spaces.   (#)

My # mark indicates that you have made a spacing error. Some of
the rules for spaces: Place two blank spaces after the period or
other closing punctuation at the end of a sentence. We insert two
blank spaces after all of the periods within each of the Works
Cited listings. Place a single blank space between two words in
a sentence. Be sure to leave one blank space after commas, like
that. If you do not,see what happens. The same rule applies to
colons: leave one space afterwards; you also leave one blank space
after semicolons, not two. You should leave a blank space after
numbers followed by closing parentheses, 1) like that, rather than
2)like that. You do not leave a space before the punctuation ,
only after. When you type a three-period ellipsis, use four spaces
to separate the three periods, like . . . this, rather than putting
the periods together like...this. You should not leave blank spaces
just inside quotation marks, parentheses, or brackets; these marks
should be closed up against the words they enclose, (like this)
rather than (like this). After an abbreviation's period, you must
use a single blank space: "Mr. Dickens," not "Mr. Dickens." In
parenthetical notes, leave a single space between the closing quotes
and the parenthetical note "that follows, like this" (Jones 54).
Leave two blank spaces between the period and the documentary note
at the end of a long quotation.

    Do not put blank spaces inside quotation marks " like this " or
within parentheses (like this); quotes and parentheses should be
closed up around the words they enclose "like" (this).

    I think of the blank space almost as a white letter--it is the
null letter, the act of placing a blank space in a place. The blank
space is a language object just as a letter or punctuation mark is
a language object. The blank space has meaning; changes in spacing
can cause changes in interpretation. Again: We normally put a
single space between words in a sentence, a single space

after colons and semicolons, a single space between Mr. and Name, and two blank spaces after the closing punctuation of each sentence.

One exception to this rule is when you are using quotation marks; then you put the closing quotation marks immediately after the period, "like this." A second exception is if the period is used after an abbreviation or initial: B. F. Skinner was here! In this case, only one space follows the initial's period.

The MLA rules permit the teacher to decide whether to use one or two blank spaces between sentences; we will use two.

Here is another lengthy explanation that would be impossible without an archive. With an archive, this copy and paste takes no more time than any other. A long comment about spaces is required, I think, because the space is invisible. With Courier, a double-space is twice as long as a single space, and this makes a spacing error in Courier highly visible, so long as the paper is ragged right rather than justified on the right margin.

```
Space correctly in documentation.  (#)
Space correctly before parenthetical notes for long and short
quotations.  My # mark means that you have made a spacing error in a
parenthetical documentary note.  Remember that spaces are language
objects, just as letters are.  You have to get them right.  When you
use a short quotation, first give the quotation in quotation marks,
and skip a single space before the documentary note "like this"
(Thompson 78).  "Do not omit the space like this"(Thompson 78) or
put two spaces "like this"  (Thompson 78).  See the difference?
        On long quotations place two spaces after the period at
        the end of the quotation before you type the documentary
        note, like this.  (Thompson 78)
```

Here is a more focused comment about spaces in parentheticals. I wanted to have this option when the longer previous comment did not seem to be required. All other things being equal, shorter is better. There is no reason to tax and exhaust a student with an endless comment if the student's clarity is only slightly out of focus.

Type two blank spaces after closing punctuation marks.   (#)
My # mark means that you have a spacing error after a period at the
end of a sentence, after a period at the end of a long quotation, or
after a period in the Works Cited.   In punctuating your sentences,
remember to place two blank spaces after the period (or other
closing punctuation such as a question mark) at the end of each
sentence--not one space, and not three.   In other words hit the
space bar of your computer keyboard two times before you begin
typing the next sentence.   Like that. Not like that.   Or that.

   We also use two spaces after the period at the end of a long
quotation.   You type the period, space twice, and then type the
parenthetical notation.   (Like that) and not. (Like that), see?

   The same principle applies to the periods in the Works Cited
listings; put two blank spaces after each period.   The result looks
like this:

   Johnson, James.   *Ten Ways to Skin a Metaphor*.   London,
         Cooper, 1993.

Here is another more focused comment that can be used to help a student who
is not using two spaces at critical points.

Use continuous underlining.

<u>Please use continuous underlining</u> <u>rather</u> <u>than</u> <u>word</u> <u>underlining</u>.
When you underline a group of words, such as the title of a book,
I would rather you use one continuous underline, rather than
leaving spaces between the words. This gives a cleaner, less busy
appearance to the paper, and after all, the spaces between the words
are part of the title, just as the letters are. In other words a
book title should look like <u>The Call of the Wild</u> rather than <u>The</u>
<u>Call</u> <u>of</u> <u>the</u> <u>Wild</u>. These days our computer word processors can make
true italics, so we no longer have to underline in most cases.

This comment is on the verge of being archaic because underlining is no longer
used in an MLA paper under ordinary circumstances, but it is impossible to
rule out all cases where underlining might be the only option. Underlining
might be required in order to make a point, or to discuss underlining itself as I
am here, or for some other reason that one does not anticipate, so for that rare
occasion when underlining reappears, here is the comment.

Do not underline inappropriate punctuation.

When a comma or period follows something that you have underlined, such as the title of a book, remember that the following punctuation is not a part of the title, and should not be underlined; you would not do it <u>this way,</u> you would do it <u>this way</u>. "I read <u>Hamlet</u>." is correct, but "I read <u>Hamlet."</u> is not, because the period is not part of the title. Also incorrect would be: "Freud's masterpiece, <u>The Interpretation of Dreams,</u> was a landmark in intellectual history"; the comma should not be underlined. Remember this point when you do the Works Cited listings; do not let the underline sneak underneath the period that follows each book title.

Again, this comment is on the verge of being unnecessary, though it was an important comment for me for many years when every student paper contained underlining. Now that word processors are omnipresent and advanced—able to render true italics—we use italics instead of underlining.

I suppose it is worth noting that a comma can be in italics, and so there are cases where a comma should not be italicized, just as it should not have been underlined. Can you see the tiny difference in these two commas?

Wrong: We read *Treasure Island,* and we enjoyed it.

Right: We read *Treasure Island*, and we enjoyed it.

The point is only the book title, not the punctuation that comes after it, should be either underlined or italicized.

88

James,

Thank you for this interesting paper on how the painter Caravaggio's outlaw lifestyle influenced the dark look of his paintings. I learned so much from your paper; I had never before heard of the term *tenebrism*, the technique Caravaggio used for shifting light tones abruptly, and I had no idea that he was personally so bellicose and aggressive. Do you think he was actually guilty of murder? There are of course some problems that you need to address if you want to get a top grade on your next paper, so let us look at some of the issues that still need attention. Your paper has some departures from what we would call academic style.

Page 2. See the awk symbol.
Use natural-sounding language. A sentence such as "This idea supports the theory of Praeger" sounds unnatural and artificial. We would never say, in normal communication, "He saw the dog of Bob"; we would say, "He saw Bob's dog." Similarly, even in a formal research paper, you should write, "This idea supports Praeger's theory." You should not be colloquial, or descend into slang, but your language should be comfortable--correctly comfortable.

Avoid contractions in formal writing. There is nothing incorrect about the grammar of a contraction, but the contraction is not in keeping with the serious intellectual tone of a formal essay. Contractions suggest that one is in a hurry and does not wish to write out each word separately. Of course, if there are contractions in a quotation you use, then you leave the contraction alone; I am only referring to the use of contractions in sentences you write yourself.

Follow the rules for blank spaces. (#)
My # mark indicates that you have made a spacing error. Some of the rules for spaces: Place two blank spaces after the period or other closing punctuation at the end of a sentence. We insert two blank spaces

Comments about Style

```
Avoid unnatural wording.
Avoid clichés.
Avoid colloquial words, a lot, slang . . .
Please avoid contractions.
Use the word and, not + or &.
Please avoid etc., etcetera.
Please avoid passive voice verb constructions.
Avoid awkward wording.  (awk)
Do not address the reader as "you."
Write graceful segues to introduce your quotations.
Please write out numbers.
Do not be wordy; make each word count.  (wdy)
```

Academic style is more subtle than other elements a student must master in academic writing. The properties of academic voice are more nuanced, more organic, more cultural, more quiet than other elements a student must learn to perceive.

Part of the problem is that almost nothing in the ordinary world either teaches or reinforces academic language. Students who do not read serious nonfiction on their own may never encounter academic language at all. It is nowhere to be found on popular radio stations, television programs, or films. It is not used by students in the hallway, and it may be rare even in the classroom. Mass-produced textbooks, for example, are not academic; they avoid academic language at every level: the vocabulary, the length of sentences, the complexity of explanation, the reliance on text itself—ordinary textbooks do not acquaint students with academic style.

This section presents some of the comments I developed to help students acquire a sense of academic style.

```
Avoid unnatural wording.
Use natural-sounding language.  A sentence such as "This idea
supports the theory of Praeger" sounds unnatural and artificial.  We
would never say, in normal communication, "He saw the dog of Bob";
we would say, "He saw Bob's dog."  Similarly, even in a formal
research paper, you should write, "This idea supports Praeger's
theory."  You should not be colloquial, or use contractions, or
descend into slang, but your language should be graceful and
comfortable--correctly comfortable.
```

Unnatural, awkward phrasing seems to be the symptom of students who feel the shock wave of real academic writing. Struggling to write with a voice they have never known, they construct odd sentences that do not read well, even if the sentences are grammatically correct in a technical sense. We have to be sympathetic and gentle about the matter. Suddenly, a student is told not to use contractions, not to use colloquial words that he or she did not even know were colloquial, not to use clichés when the very idea of a cliché is new, and it takes time for the student to do enough academic reading and writing to get it untangled. In the hubbub and noise of these standards, students who are trying hard to sound grown-up and scholarly can create unnatural sentences.

This comment would often be the beginning of an explanation; I would add on to the bottom, going over the student's actual sentence and explaining in a nice way why the sentence sounded unnatural or awkward.

Avoid clichés.

Please use original language rather than clichés. In a formal paper you should avoid using all clichés, which are standard phrases that everyone knows, such as "the upper hand," "ups and downs," "way ahead of his time," "to stand in his shoes," "in this day and age," "the bottom line," "at the end of the day," "pretty far along," "the world as we know it," or "told him to his face." You would not say, for example, that you can almost "reach out and touch" the characters in Homer's vivid poems because that phrase is a tired cliché that we have heard before. Express your idea in your own original words: In Homer's vivid poems the characters seem so real that you feel you could touch their faces. See? You would not say that Hemingway's characters "give it their best shot." You can use the same idea, but by putting it in original language, you make it much more effective: Hemingway's characters struggle honestly with the problems they face. In general if you have heard a phrase before, then do not use it. Avoid all prefab, ready-made phrases and sayings. Make up your own phrases and metaphors; find your own ways to say things.

Here again we need to—I will use a cliché—stand in the student's shoes. There is little in ordinary life that would inform a student that a popular phrase should not be used in certain contexts. In fact the opposite is true; popular phrases are popular. Suddenly a student who has received approval for using the latest in-words is told that they are not allowed; fine, but the student has never known any alternative because the student has done no real nonfiction reading. The problem of clichés is a subtle one that can take time to address. Encourage students to ask you about any language they think may be a cliché.

Avoid colloquial words, a lot, slang . . .

Choose academic, not conversational, words. Please do not use slang or inappropriately informal language in a formal paper. The words you choose should be good, ordinary academic words; you should not use lofty, stilted, or pompous diction. Avoid saying that we can "relate to" a book; rather, we can understand it. You should not say that Shakespeare was a "heavy guy," or that he wrote "a lot" of plays. In fact, please completely avoid using the term "a lot" in formal papers. Instead of "a lot," use a clearer word, such as "many." Shakespeare wrote many plays. Even a sentence such as "Aristotle thought that the best life should contain some tremendously great item" is too colloquial; it sounds like chatty conversation rather than the disciplined, sedate tone of a research paper.

Reading is the beginning of writing. Often, with these first research papers, we are asking students to write in a language they have never known. It is almost no exaggeration to say that *all* of their socially acquired language conventions are inappropriate and unusable. It takes reading experience to develop an ear for the conventions of academic style, and this is one reason why research papers are far superior to asking students to do non-research academic essays—research papers force students, often for the first time in their lives, to read massive amounts of actual academic nonfiction. As students do research for paper after paper, they become attuned to the sound and voice of academic writing. Research forces them to read, and reading teaches them the tones, notes, and melody of academic language. You have to read it to get it.

```
Please avoid contractions.
Avoid contractions such as can't, isn't, don't and it's in formal
writing.  There is nothing incorrect about the grammar of a
contraction, but the contraction is not in keeping with the serious
intellectual style of a formal essay.  Contractions suggest that one
is in a hurry and does not wish to write out each word separately.
Of course, if there are contractions in a quotation you use, then
you leave the contraction alone; I am only referring to the use of
contractions in sentences you write yourself.
```

Students are often incredulous about this standard, asking sincerely what is wrong with contractions and why they are not allowed to use them in a formal paper. It is not that they do not understand, it is only that they have not yet thought about it. Would they want their report cards to be full of contractions? Their diploma? Their marriage certificate? Would they want the President to speak in contractions and slang at state dinners? Contractions are not bad grammar; they are casual style. Think about it: contractions are, by their very nature, blurred. Blurry is exactly what we do not want in a research paper; it should be crisp and sharp.

```
Use the word and, not + or &.
Use the word and rather than a plus (+) or an ampersand (&).
Sometimes students think that and, +, and & are all acceptable or
interchangeable, and they may write about "Socrates & Plato" or
about "Socrates + Plato."  But pluses and ampersands are not words;
a plus is only a mathematical symbol representing addition, and
an ampersand has very limited uses and should not be substituted
casually for the word and.  In a formal paper we write primarily
with words--not symbols, not contractions, not abbreviations.  Write
with words.
```

I remember being astonished that I had to correct this. I just could not believe that it was not obvious to every student that you do not cut corners this way in a formal paper. After all, a formal paper is not scribbles, and students have never seen a plus or an ampersand used instead of a conjunction in any book; even in mathematics books, pluses are not used as conjunctions in explanatory paragraphs. Where would students acquire this idea? After correcting this error year after year, often from good students, I finally realized that this is another symptom of growing up in a culture that is overwhelmingly informal, a culture where formal language is almost absolutely absent from student experience.

The only response can be to try to be wise and understanding about it, and patiently correct this problem until it recedes.

```
Please avoid etc., etcetera.
Instead of putting the abbreviation etc. at the end of a list,
say something concrete and specific using real words, such as "and
other forms of incompetence."  Write with complete words, not vague
suggestions.  Do not give the reader the impression that you do
not have time to be complete or specific; in a formal paper, you DO
have time to spell things out.  Furthermore, even if you type out
etcetera, you would still be better off to say something explanatory
instead; the reader may or may not know what you mean by etcetera;
do not take that chance; say what you mean.  It is better to be sure
that you are clear than to assume that you are clear.
```

The use of *etc.* is similar to many other violations of style; it is a short-cut, a vague gesture that communicates: "I am not going to take my time to be specific about the details, so you just have to know what I mean."

This and similar comments reveal one of the glories of the academic research paper; the process teaches students to be complete, to take whatever time is required to say the words that are necessary. An academic paper is not the equivalent of fast food; the reader of an academic paper is not going to drive by; he or she is going to move in, and the place has to be ready.

Please avoid passive voice verb constructions.

Instead of saying "What has been shown by Homer," say "What Homer has shown." Instead of saying "Dickens was honored by the Society," say "The Society honored Dickens." Instead of "Some examples are given by Durant," say "Durant gives four examples." Use an active voice verb and a direct object, rather than a passive voice verb and a prepositional phrase. Active voice gives your writing energy, vigor, and impact, whereas passive voice is lacking in force.

Passive voice can be a problem in the sentences you use to introduce quotations, where there is a tendency to say something such as, "It is written by William Simon that . . ." Active voice would be better: "William Simon notes that . . ."

Every clause requires the writer to look deliberately at the verb. Even though the sentence is about the subject, the verb is the center of the connections that hold the sentence together. The very strength of the sentence is at stake in the verb. The verb must agree with the subject in number. It must be a well-chosen word that does not need adverbs to stand it back up. It must be in a logical tense and parallel with other verbs in the paragraph. It wants to be beside its subject rather than reaching across a prepositional phrase. Finally, an action verb should usually be active voice so that the subject gets the fun of doing something, rather than just standing around. At the heart of writing good sentences, there is a great deal of verb-think.

```
Avoid awkward wording.  (awk)
I have written awk to indicate that the wording of a sentence is
awkward.  This does not mean that the sentence is incomplete (a
fragment) or that it is necessarily very confusing, but it does mean
that the words are not in a normal order--they do not read smoothly,
gracefully, or naturally.  Putting words and phrases in a graceful,
pleasant order is an important art.  Even though a reader can, with
some effort, understand awkward writing, he or she will not enjoy it.
Awkward sentences slow the reader's progress and distract his mind
from your ideas.  Write your sentences so that they are easy and
nice to read.
```

As you have seen, I have addressed this issue in a number of different ways already. I often found that although I had a comment that was more or less usable, I was not content with the comment I already had, and I wanted to write a new option that would put the matter a little differently. Part of the reason is that these matters are devilishly difficult to articulate, and one wants to try again. Having a variety of comments helps.

Do not address the reader as "you."
This is a formal paper that explores an idea; it is not a private
communication that is addressed to a single individual. Therefore,
it has a different tone; the reader is not expecting suddenly to
read a reference to himself or herself; the reader is expecting all
of the sentences to be about Hercules, or Existentialism, or Dante,
or *Song of Myself*. Instead of writing, "You have to remember that
dreaming alone never accomplished anything," write "Perhaps dreams
alone never accomplished anything." Leave out the second person
pronoun.

The objection to addressing the reader as "you" is related to the objection to any form of self-reference in a research paper. The research paper is a form of essay with a connecting thesis. The goal is to point the reader's mind to the content of the thesis and keep it there. The sharpest strategy is to talk about, and only about, the thesis—always. Any time we break the hypnotic spell of the thesis and slap the reader with distracting side references to ourselves, to himself, to the paper as a paper, to quotations as quotations, the reader's concentration suffers.

We see here another key to a quality that great papers possess, a feeling of simplicity, a quality of being easy to understand. This simplicity is advanced; simplicity is one of the last things that students achieve. Bad papers are much harder to understand than good papers. One of the secrets to simplicity is to have one focus.

Write graceful segues to introduce your quotations.

Do you know the sentence you write just before a quotation in order to lead in to the quotation? Well, let us call that a segue, pronounced SEG-way. A common problem that beginning writers have is the inability to write a graceful segue.

There are three common varieties of the bad segue: one is the boring repetitive segue, in which the student uses the same phrase to introduce every quotation (He stated . . ., He stated . . ., He stated . . ., *ad nauseam*).

A second special variety of the bad segue is the verbose, awkwardly worded segue, such as "This is what Dickens says when he quotes the statement that says . . ."

A third variety of the bad segue is the passive voice segue: "It is stated by Richmond Lattimore that . . ." Active voice would be better: "Richmond Lattimore states that . . ."

Please work on the economy, variety, and the grace of your segues. Use few words, make them sound natural and pleasant, and vary them. Examples include such phrases as, "Dickens explained: In Shakespeare's words: Perhaps Steinbeck described it best: Hemingway disagreed: James pointed out an interesting corollary: " and so on. You want the thoughts to flow naturally and pleasantly from your text into the quote.

Another reason that a paper can lose its power over the reader is that the writing suddenly becomes unpleasant and knotted. This makes the reader stop thinking about Alexander or gravitation, and turns the reader's eyes to the flat, white paper in front of him. We do not want the paper to suffer from such disruptions of flow, and one of the most likely locations for a paper to crash is in the introduction to a quotation. Papers full of repetitive, awkward, verbose, or passive segues will break the reader's link to the content.

Please write out numbers.

Rather than using numerals to indicate one- or two-digit numbers
in your paper, it is best to write the numbers from one to ninety-
nine as words; from 100 up, when you begin three digits, you may
use numerals. This is true of dates; you may use 1776, even though
it is made of numerals. In most cases you should avoid numerals
in fractions; use words for simple fractions such as one third:
"As many as one third of the participants had no illness at all."
The reason we avoid smaller numerals is that our work is literary
rather than mathematical in nature, and so we use words rather than
numbers. Instead of writing "When Sophocles was 28," write "When
Sophocles was twenty-eight . . ."

We write out numbers for the same reason that we do not use pluses or
ampersands; a research paper is a construction of words. We do not want the
reader's mind to be switching systems back and forth from words to numbers
to abbreviations to signs; we just want the writing, as much of it as possible,
to be a beautiful sequence of words. Words unify.

Do not be wordy; make each word count. (wdy)

The proofreading abbreviation *wdy* means "wordy." It is important to express your ideas in a lean, effective way, without using needless words or being repetitive. What is the difference, for example, between "the population as a whole," and the population? Is there a population as a part? It is easy to let indefensible words slither into your sentences. A wordy sentence such as "He had used it almost all the time when he would engage in an intellectual or even an every day discussion about any sort of topic that he would like to know more about" should be edited: "He had used it in intellectual and everyday discussions." Good writing style requires eliminating all words that do not carry their weight. As Carl Sandburg said, you have to write one word at a time. In practice, this means not writing with phrases or clauses whose internal contents you do not examine, but making a decision about each word individually.

Wordiness is a serious problem. Wordy writing can be exasperating and repulsive, even when the grammar is correct. Emphasize clean writing.

This comment calls attention to one of the primary differences between what bad writers do and what good writers do: the unit of writing. When a bad writer writes, the writing gushes out in clumps of clauses; the writer is not really thinking about the sentences at all; he or she is thinking about the content, looking through the sentences as through a thin mist. When a good writer writes, the unit of expression is not a clump of unexamined clauses; a good writer also cares about the content, but for that very reason the good writer wants the sentences to be true, to capture the reality of the content, and so the good writer writes one slow, careful sentence at a time, checking each word and eliminating words that clutter the sentence. The good writer tries to create a sentence that exactly mirrors the content. To write about a dog, first think about the dog, but then think about the sentence about the dog.

Once the words are true and right, additional words damage the sentence. A key to great proofreading is to remove unnecessary words that add nothing to your ideas.

96

Sarah,

I enjoyed your paper on Hannibal's strategy at the battle of Cannae. I did not know that Hannibal was outnumbered four-to-one, or that it was one of the largest armies the Romans ever put in the field. You chose concrete facts and details that make your writing vivid. I also thought your essay structure and paragraphing were clear and continuous, and I loved the careful, patient conclusion you wrote. This is an advanced paper. Let us look at a few details that still need attention:

Page 1. Study the usage of *affect* and *effect*.
As verbs, *affect* means influence, and *effect* means cause. We are affected by other people, and a good idea can effect a solution. To influence is to affect: Hannibal was affected by other men, not effected by them. As nouns, the words are also different: an effect is the result of a cause, and an affect is a pretension in one's behavior. If one thing has an *effect* (noun) on another, then it *affects* (verb) it. This is a detail that educated people know, so you must gain control over it.

Do not address the reader as "you."
This is a formal paper that explores an idea; it is not a private communication that is addressed to a single individual. Therefore, it has a different tone; the reader is not expecting suddenly to read a reference to himself or herself; the reader is expecting all of the sentences to be about Hercules, or Existentialism, or Dante, or *Song of Myself*. Instead of writing, "You have to remember that dreaming alone never accomplished anything," write "Perhaps dreams alone never accomplished anything." Leave out the second person pronoun.

Know the difference between *less* and *fewer*. We use *less* for things that do not come in countable units: less sugar. We use *fewer* for things that we can count: fewer pencils, fewer metaphors, fewer ideas.

Comments about Usage

Please learn the difference between *accepted* and *excepted*.

Study the usage of *affect* and *effect*.

Use *affected*, not *impacted*.

Use the prepositions *between* and *among* correctly.

Use *first* and *second*, not *firstly* and *secondly*.

Do not substitute *hopefully* for "I hope."

Use the words *human*, *person*, and *individual* correctly.

Do not confuse *hung* and *hanged*.

Do not confuse *ideas* with *ideals*.

Do not confuse *its* and *it's*.

Know the difference between *less* and *fewer*.

Avoid *like* when you mean *as*.

Be careful using *man*, *mankind*, and *his*.

Do not confuse *principles* with *principals*.

Avoid the phrase "relate to."

The reason is not *because*; the reason is *that*.

Please do not confuse *then* with *than*.

Use *there*, *their*, and *they're* correctly.

Please learn the difference between *to*, *two*, and *too*.

Nothing can be very unique.

Use *who*, *that*, and *which* gracefully.

Usage is a more approachable problem than style because it is more concrete, confined, and identifiable. There are nameable items and lucid rules, and this makes it easier for students new to academic language to understand and eliminate common usage errors. It would be possible to create a long list of usage errors, and I do have such a list in this and other writing books (see the reference section at the back of the book), but the errors you see above are the ones that resulted in archived comments. These were the repeat offenders.

```
Please learn the difference between accepted and excepted.
To be accepted is to be admitted: one is accepted by a college.  To
be excepted is to be made an exception: One person is excepted from
rules that apply to all others.  A business might accept all credit
cards except Mastercharge.
```

Many usage problems are caused by homophones or near homophones. Here is a perfect example; a student may never have noticed the slight difference in pronunciation of the first vowel. This is another case of an error that a student has to stare down until it collapses. What makes the problem serious is that these are not unusual words; they are common, so a student who gets this wrong is going to get it wrong frequently. Notice that this problem is one that would be barely noticeable in spoken English; it surfaces in writing.

Study the usage of *affect* and *effect*.

As verbs, *affect* means influence, and *effect* means cause. We are affected by other people, and a good idea can effect a solution. To influence is to affect: Hannibal was affected by other men, not effected by them. As nouns, the words are also different: an effect is the result of a cause, and an affect is a pretension in one's behavior. If one thing has an effect (noun) on another, then it affects (verb) it. This is a detail that educated people know, so you must gain control over it.

A disgusting variation of this error involves the noun *impact*. It has become common to use *impact* as a verb and to say, "This event impacted me" instead of "This event affected me." Do not do that because that usage suggests an unpleasant medical condition. Use *impact* as a noun; when something has an impact on you, say that it affects you.

The *affect-effect* usage problem is much like the confusion between *accept* and *except*, except that here there is an alien intruder that enters the scene: *impact*. Although the dictionary does indicate that impact can be used as a verb in some situations, we do not want students to write sentences such as, "His father's imprisonment for debt impacted young Charles Dickens."

```
Use affected, not impacted.
It is best to use the word impact only as a noun, and not as a verb,
in discussing the effect of individuals on history.  When we say that
x "impacted" y, this usage has an unfortunate, unpleasant medical
connotation that is undesirable.  The right word is affected.  We
affect others, rather than impact them, and when we affect them, this
has an impact.
```

This comment is a more focused version of the previous comment about *affect* and *effect*. There are students who do not confuse *affect* with *effect* but who still say that the election defeat impacted Davy Crockett. The use of *impacted* as a verb is now so popular in conversation and television that the street usage is likely to persist, but we can still teach students to be more pleasant in academic writing.

Use the prepositions *between* and *among* correctly.
Something is between two, but it is among three or more. Between
you and me, this usage error is just one among many. The word
between comes through Old English from the older Germanic *be*, by,
and *tween*, two. We still retain the sense of *tween* in our English
word *twain*, as in "Never the twain [two] shall meet." Jane Austen
did not choose between five titles; she chose among five, but after
she narrowed the choice to two titles, she had to choose between
them.

The prepositions *between* and *among* are not homophones, so this error is easier to correct for any student who decides to focus on it. What makes this one especially logical and therefore easy is the etymology of *between*, by two. The alternative, *among*, comes from an Old English word *genang* which meant assemblage.

Use *first* and *second*, not *firstly* and *secondly*.
If you are enumerating elements in your essay, use *first* and *second*, rather than *firstly* and *secondly*. The latter terms with their *-ly* suffix have a supercilious, pedantic ring to them that is obnoxious. In fact Thomas Hardy even satirized the use of such language in one of his poems, "Channel Firing." In the poem a skeleton wakes up in the grave and muses about someone he knows: "Parson Thirdly."

Furthermore, you should consider whether you even want to use the recommended words *first*, *second*, and so forth, which seem cold and mechanical, rather than graceful and more specific language such as "Another reason why Charlotte Brontë explored the theme is . . ."

Words can acquire connotations that make them undesirable, and the words *firstly*, *secondly*, *thirdly*, have acquired the odd odor of the pedant. Yes, these words can be used to introduce the paragraphs of the body of an essay, and they do impart a measure of clarity, but they are tedious. Thomas Hardy's 1914 poem "Channel Firing," by the way, is an extraordinary poem. The seventh quatrain of "Channel Firing" is:

> And many a skeleton shook his head.
> "Instead of preaching forty year,"
> My neighbor Parson Thirdly said,
> "I wish I had stuck to pipes and beer."

Parson *Thirdly*—ouch.

```
Do not substitute hopefully for "I hope."
Do not use the adverb hopefully to mean "I hope."  Hopefully should
be used to mean just what it says: full of hope.  A person could run
hopefully toward the finish line or look hopefully toward a parent
for approval.  Instead of saying, "Hopefully, there will be enough
porridge," say, "I hope there will be enough porridge."  This is a
widespread usage error, but please avoid it.
```

The *hopefully* error is one of the most egregious errors in spoken English; rare is the person who does not breezily introduce a sentence with the dreaded word, followed by a comma. The convention sounds so chatty and sophomoric, you would think it would be rare to find it in a formal research paper, but students seem drawn to the error in sermonizing sentences such as "Hopefully, we will all remember Charles Dickens's ideas." I hope that students will not sermonize so hopefully.

```
Use the words human, person, individual carefully.
Be sensitive to word nuances and contexts.  The term a human or
the plural humans is more anthropological than philosophical and
is not the way we would normally refer to people collectively.  In
anthropology it is normal to talk about "a human": we might say that
a hominid was a human but an anthropoid is not, but we would say that
an ethical life is important to a person, or to an individual.  Often
the best replacement for human is human being: "For more than two
thousand years, human beings have developed philosophies of ethics."
That is better than "Humans have developed . . . ."
```

This problem could be included in the section about style; it is a question of the ear, of hearing how something sounds and knowing whether it is the right choice for the context. Students who have done large amounts of personal reading, especially of nonfiction, will be less likely to take the wrong tone. Fortunately, this is a fairly concrete choice to explain: usually *human beings* is better than *humans*.

Do not confuse *hung* and *hanged*.
When someone is executed by hanging, we say that he is *hanged*.
Clothes are hung; people are hanged. Paintings are hung. After his
ill-fated attack on Harper's Ferry, Virginia, John Brown was hanged.
One commonly hears it said that someone has been hung, but when that
is the case, the person can walk away afterwards, dry.

I have not yet been hanged, though rumors persist. Unlike the *affect-effect* distinction, the *hanged-hung* distinction is a grain of knowledge that one does not need in every paper, but when you do need it, you do, because the misuse renders a sentence ridiculous.

Do not confuse *ideas* with *ideals*.

Please notice the difference between ideas and ideals. Ideas are concepts, thoughts. We could discuss the philosophical ideas of Friedrich Nietzsche. Ideals are perfect standards, goals to be attained, concepts of excellence or perfection, such as those that Thomas Jefferson used to express the highest dreams of American democracy. Both ideas and ideals are mental, but we debate ideas while striving for the ideal. There is no such word as *idears*, though we hear that mispronunciation in conversation. We often see *ideal* in its adjective form, as in, "These were not ideal conditions."

Because students often discuss ideas in research papers, the difference between ideas and ideals is a lurking problem. A student who is new to academic language (as a result of limited reading experience) may think that *ideal* sounds more scholarly than *idea* and use it in an effort to give his or her paper a mature tone. More often than I expected, I had to correct this usage.

Do not confuse *its* and *it's*.

Please learn the difference between the word *its* and the contraction *it's*. The first is a possessive adjective: Every dog has its day. Since *its* is a possessive adjective like *my* or *our*, it is already possessive and does not have an apostrophe to make it possessive. The second, *it's*, is a contraction of a pronoun, *it*, and a verb, *is*: It's a profound idea. In this case the apostrophe replaces the missing *i* in the word *is*. Remember that in formal papers we do not use contractions in our own writing because they are inherently informal, and so you will not use *it's*, even correctly, in a formal paper.

From my experience of decades grading academic writing, I would nominate this error—is it a usage error or a punctuation error?—as one of the most frequent. The most egregious form of the error is when students attempt to use *it's* as a possessive adjective because they think that possessives have apostrophes. Not only is this an error that many students make, it is also an error that is resistant to correction (1) because the two alternatives are perfect homophones, (2) because there is a tradition of possessive apostrophes, and (3) it is an error that mutates a sentence into a gross laughingstock. The center of destruction is the fact that the *it's* error transmogrifies a subservient pronoun into a major subject pronoun with verb, but a subject/verb set that means nothing. Like a virus-infected cell, the sentence bursts.

Every dog has it's day

means

Every dog has it is day.

The *it's* error is stealthy and destructive.

```
Know the difference between less and fewer.
We use less for things that do not come in countable units: less
sugar.  We use fewer for things that we can count: fewer pencils,
fewer metaphors, fewer ideas.
```

The colloquial standard is to say *less* at all times, and so students will write that after three hours of battle, the defenders at the Alamo had less bullets. That is the habit that students most likely bring to the assignment, and many students may not have used *fewer* ever. Unlike the *it's* error, this error does not destroy the meaning of a sentence, but it does ripple the sensibility of anyone who knows the expected usage. The good news is that *less* and *fewer* are not homophones, which makes them easier to differentiate, and this is a comparatively easy error to eliminate with incessant correction.

```
Avoid using like when you mean as.
Best academic practice is to use like as a preposition and not to
use it as a conjunction instead of as.  Do as I say, not like I say.
Perplexity is as Plato says, not like Plato says.  Xenophon wrote the
Anabasis as he would normally write something.  Correct usage of like
would be as the first word of a prepositional phrase, like any other
preposition: The moon was like a face.  Edward had a shovel like
mine.  Like a great flood, Darius's army swept over the plain.
        Like can also be used as an adjective, as when we say that two
people are of "like minds."  In this case like is a form of alike.
```

There are many uses for *like*, such as when we use it as a verb, but the substitution of *like* for *as* as a conjunction is the problem spot. Dorothy Parker is said to have been so repulsed by this error that when she was reviewing a book, she would stop reading and throw the book into the trash if she found a *like*/*as* error. The Parker story does illustrate a sort of impatience that exists in the academic world; scholars have gone to the trouble to learn the details of correct usage, and they expect other writers to as well.

Be careful using *man*, *mankind*, and *his*.
In the past we used the nouns *man* and *mankind*, and even the possessive pronoun *his*, to refer to all human beings, both male and female. We would say things such as, "From the beginning of time, man has adapted to his environment." The problem with calling everyone *man* is that half of humanity is woman, so the wording did not reflect the truth. Today, our sensitivities are more precise, and we avoid defaulting to the masculine gender when we intend to express something that also includes women. Other terms, such as *human beings*, *humanity*, *persons*, and even the compound pronouns such as *his or her* sound more accurate and more fair. In a formal research paper, it is important to express yourself in a manner that is both precise and just.

This is a detail that young writers must learn to incorporate, and yet doing so can throw the writer into a dilemma, having to choose between justice and grace. It becomes stylistically tedious, for example, to fill an essay with a conglomeration of compound pronouns (he and she, him and her); the flow is disrupted. Usually, there is a graceful way to work around the problem. Instead of saying either *man* or *he and she*, we can often use a more focused, concrete reference, such as "the population of ancient Crete." As in so many writing issues, the problem is solved by moving from the general to the specific.

Do not confuse principles with principals.

Principle is a noun that means a basic truth, a standard, or a rule, but the noun *principal* means a person who presides or stars in an important role. *Principal* can also be an adjective, meaning primary. We could say that the principles of morality make each person the principal of his or her own life; that is the principal principle.

Here is another usage problem caused by homophones. Like other homophone problems, this one will only be solved by concentrated attention and serious intention. If the student wants to learn the detail, he or she can learn it. With the archive available, we can easily paste this comment into a student's papers, as many times as it takes.

Avoid the phrase "relate to."

The phrase "relate to" is a vague cliché, so vague as to be
meaningless in most sentences because there are so many ways of
relating to things. Be specific. Write with detail. Instead of
saying that many people relate to J.D. Salinger's character Holden
Caulfield, say that many people understand Holden, or that they
find that Holden's struggles remind them of their own struggles,
or something specific like that. To say we relate to Holden is
vague. In what way do we relate? Do we mean that we feel the same
alienation from conventional society that Holden feels? Do we have
dreams similar to Holden's dream of being the catcher in the rye? Do
we love our little brothers and sisters as Holden does? Do we feel
that Holden's language expresses our own view of the world? Do we
feel ourselves losing our emotional or psychological health as Holden
does? There are so many kinds of relationships that simply to say
one thing relates to another is almost to say nothing; you have to
use a specific word that identifies that specific relationship.

This comment explores another case of the tone-deafness that results from a
bookless life, and it is a common problem in student writing. Students hear
relate to every day in conversation, but they never know there is an alternative
or that *relate to* is only used in popular slang because the alternative language
is in serious nonfiction. They have not noticed that *relate to* emerges in casual
sentences such as, "Cool, man, I can relate to that!" We simply have to teach
students to hear this, to help them develop an ear for it.

The other element to be emphasized here is that specific words, specific details,
are always more interesting and vivid than generalities.

The reason is not *because*; the reason is *that*.
When you are explaining what the reason is for something, use the
word *that* instead of the word *because*. The reason Poseidon disliked
the Trojans was that (not because) Zeus favored them. This is a
standard of usage because when you say *the reason is because*, you are
repeating yourself; you already said it was a reason, so you do not
need the word *because*; just say, "The reason we eliminate adjectives
is that they clog sentences." An alternative is to eliminate the
word *reason* instead and say, "We eliminate adjectives because they
clog sentences." Use *because* alone or *reason . . . that*.

This comment focuses on a logical operator; the offense that occurs in *the reason is because* is an offense of mind, a redundancy that is rejected as tedious and without logical value. Part of the ideal of good writing is that the flow of thought clicks, the parts of the logic work together, and there is no useless or redundant part, no inoperative part. In addition to its other elements, academic writing is a manifestation of logic.

```
Please do not confuse then with than.
The first, then, is an adverb that refers to past time: I did it
then.  Then can also mean "in that case": If it is not true, then
is it false?  The second word, than, is a conjunction: This rule is
easier to explain than it is to apply.  Hannibal wished then that he
had a larger army than the Romans.
```

Here we have near-homophones. With the casual slurs and blurs and contractions that dominate popular talk, it is even possible that a student would arrive at our assignment never having noticed that *then* and *than* are different words. It is even possible that the two words are pronounced exactly the same by the student's friends and the adults the student knows. After all, we live in a culture that says *don'tcha* instead of *don't you* and *idnit* instead of *isn't it*, and if you have not been reading books, this casual language may be all you have ever known. It can be difficult for us as instructors to gain or maintain perspective when we encounter errors like these; it is tempting to be irritated and think that the student was just being sloppy or disrespectful of the assignment. The truth may be more grave; the student may be a newcomer to the academic stratum of English. The nice thing about the archive is that we do not have to go through the tedium of explaining *then* and *than* all over again; we can copy and paste.

Use *there*, *their*, and *they're* correctly.
Please do not confuse the homophones *their*, *there*, and *they're*.
The first is a possessive pronoun, the second is an adverb, and the third is the contraction of a subject and verb. They're going to buy their lumber while they are there.

    Pronoun: We gradually unloaded their cargo.

    Adverb: We landed there, rather than at the usual quay.

    Contraction: They're not going to like this.

This error occurs in many student papers, and this is to be expected because it involves a set of triple homophones. Part of the solution is making sure that the students understand the grammar of the problem; the grammar is the difference between obtuse memorization and actual clarity, not just remembering which one to use but understanding why. Students who are taught why will understand the usage sooner and remember it more easily. Grammar is a way of thinking about language.

```
Please learn the difference between to, two, and too.
The word two is a number, usually an adjective: two hands, two feet.
The word to is either a preposition or an infinitive: to Rome, to
dream.   The word too is an adverb meaning too much or also: He was
too busy; I was too.
```

Here is another famous triple homophone, known for bedeviling student writing. We want students to see this as an elementary expectation, not as an advanced challenge. Explain this detail firmly and announce that you expect these three words to be used correctly, always.

```
Nothing can be very unique.
```

The adjective *unique* permits no degrees; something either is unique, or it is not. Unique means one-of-a-kind, literally. If something is unique, then there is only one (uni) of it in the universe. The grand canyon is unique. You are unique. Accordingly, something can not be very unique, or extremely unique, or the most unique. When you have said that it is unique, you have already said something so extreme as to be absolute.

Compared to many usage problems, this is a minor matter. It is a standard that many, even in the academic world, might not notice or know about. What makes it valuable to consider is that the violation is a result of a pointless modifier.

The difference between *unique* and *very unique* is instructive, an illustration of how modifiers (adjectives and adverbs) at least alter and often damage their objects. In particle physics the quantum theory holds that the act of observing a small particle disturbs it, so you can never know what the particle is like in its unobserved state; you can only make an estimate. I think modifying is like that, modification disturbs what it modifies, which is why the verb *modify* is a better word than *describe* to explain what an adjective or adverb does. Somehow, very unique is less unique than unique is.

Use *who*, *that*, and *which* gracefully.

Study the subtle differences among pronouns. The pronouns *who*, *that*, and *which* take some thought to use gracefully. When you are referring to persons, please use personal pronouns rather than pronouns that typically refer to inanimate objects or processes. We would do better to say, for example, that "Marcus Aurelius was a man who should not have been a ruler," rather than "Marcus Aurelius was a man that should not have been a ruler," although *that* would not be grammatically incorrect. *Who* is more personal; *that* is more objective. Elizabeth Bishop uses *that* in her poem "Visit to St. Elizabeth's" to emphasize the dehumanized lives of the patients: "These are the years and the walls and the door that shut on a boy that pats the floor." We would describe a man *who* fell but a rock *that* fell if we wanted to emphasize the humanity of the falling man.

The pronoun *which* is best used in nonessential clauses that are set off by commas. When the clause is essential, the pronoun *that* is better. So we would write, "These are the times that try men's souls," rather than "These are the times which try men's souls." Or, "I once stumbled on the steps of the library, which is a good reason to avoid libraries!"

Grammar is a way of thinking about language, and for our purposes in this text, grammar is a way of thinking about writing. Grammar lets us explain writing with a clarity that is otherwise impossible. This comment shows the power of the archive to provide extensive instruction for students; the explanation of pronouns is long, filled with examples, and expressed in terms of the grammar, which is the key to clarity. This level of feedback would be impossible without the archive.

A Final Reflection

As a whole, the comments of the archive condense down to a small center of writer's principles. Good essay structure is a unity, with the thesis, introduction, body, conclusion, paragraph integrity, and flow all contributing to that unity. Good grammar means writing in the language that a reader is expecting without disturbing the conventions of clarity and harmony that require grammar to be the way it is. Good ideas are those that are perceived as the writer's ideas, not as tedious restatements of the shallow and obvious. Good format means following the quiet principles of visual clarity established by the MLA method. Good punctuation means understanding the place of punctuation in displaying the logical segments of sentences to the reader's mind. Good style means participating in the economy, directness, and ease of academic language culture. Good usage means positioning one's mind to navigate the rapids of homophones and the sirens of popular wordings that wreck sentences.

In the end the point is the point. All of these intentions converge in the service of meaning; to express meaning requires unity, clarity, clear format, intelligent punctuation that sharpens logic, direct statement, right words, a fresh idea. It is these simple things that are mastered last. Simplicity is advanced, and simplicity cannot be learned in one paper. To get good at this, you have to have done it before—many times. By using the archive, we can provide students with a body of calm, supportive, detailed instruction that will help them develop, paper after paper, into academic writers.

97

Ellen,

Thank you for this excellent paper about Sophocles's concept of fate in *Oedipus Rex*. You discovered aspects of the problem that I had never considered, especially in the question of whether human beings can be held accountable for decisions that they are foredoomed to make. Your sentence about "divine injustice" in Greek tragedy was especially sharp, capturing the depth of the question. You also provided superb quotations from Adams and Carrigan that enhanced your thesis. Now I want to read *Oedipus Rex* again, even though we just read it in class. There are of course some problems in your paper, errors that you will not be making for long, but we need to focus on a few:

Nothing can be very unique.
The adjective *unique* permits no degrees; something either is unique, or it is not. Unique means one-of-a-kind, literally. If something is unique, then there is only one (uni) of it in the universe. The grand canyon is unique. You are unique. Accordingly, something can not be very unique, or extremely unique, or the most unique. When you have said that it is unique, you have already said something so extreme as to be absolute. Your sentence that "Oedipus found himself in a very unique dilemma" needs revision.

Do not put a comma in an ID complex sentence. (ID)
You wrote, "Oedipus had to reasses, because events were refuting him." Remember not to use a comma in an ID complex sentence such as "Socrates would not teach because he said he had nothing to teach." If the independent clause comes first, no comma: ID. If the dependent clause comes first, then put a comma: D,I. "Because he had nothing to teach, Socrates would not teach." I expect you to follow the clause punctuation rules we have studied: (I;I I,ccI D,I ID). Every time you write a sentence you must make a conscious clause punctuation decision.

Reference Section

This collection of references is taken from the *Advanced Academic Writing* series, to which this book is a supplement. Although these references are already present in the *Advanced Academic Writing* texts, they are provided here again for your convenience, so that you will not have to put this book down and look something up in another. I also want to ensure a completely consistent background of rules and standards that can be applied to my writing programs.

You will notice that many of the items in the archive of comments are included in the reference lists, but that overlap might obscure the difference; the archive makes no effort to be comprehensive; it is a collection of the most common problems, not of all problems. The archive contains only explanations that I felt compelled to save after having to type them repeatedly.

MLA FORMAT

The MLA (Modern Language Association) research paper method is the most widely adopted standard in the world, used in more high schools, colleges, and universities than any other. MLA is more standard in literary and humanities papers than in the sciences, but it is also used in those areas and is the simplest format to use when you are first learning. It has achieved this acceptance because of this clarity and simplicity. Our papers will be prepared on a computer word processor (advanced papers are not handwritten), using the MLA format exclusively, and without deviation from its standards.

1. A **one-inch margin** on all four sides of the paper.
2. The entire paper is **double-spaced**, including long quotations.
3. The text is **ragged right**, not justified.
4. One-half inch from the top of every page is a **header** with the student's name followed by the page number. There is no comma after the name.
5. There is **no separate title page**; the title information appears at the top of page one; this includes the student's name, the teacher's name, the name of the course, and the date; all of this is flush left. This is followed by the title of the paper, exactly centered.
6. The **title should not be underlined**, put in quotations, or in all-capital letters. If a book title that should be in italics is in the paper's title, then italicize only the book title.
7. Instead of footnotes, MLA documents quotations or other borrowings with **parenthetical documentation**, consisting of the author's name and the page number enclosed in parentheses, like this: (Thompson 12). The author's name in any parenthetical must appear in the alphabetical list of authors that appears on the Works Cited page. Subsequent quotations from an author may include page number only.
8. **Long quotations** of four lines or more are **indented ten spaces**. The parenthetical for a long quote comes after the period, but for a short quote it comes before.
9. Instead of a Bibliography at the end of the paper, MLA uses **Works Cited**. On the Works Cited page or pages, authors are listed alphabetically. Names in parentheticals appear in this list. Publishers in the listings are abbreviated; Random House is simply Random, Harvard University Press is Harvard UP.
10. **Do not put the paper in a separate cardboard or plastic cover**. Do not punch holes in the paper. Staple the paper in the top left corner.

PUNCTUATION RULES

In the *Advanced Academic Writing* series we reviewed punctuation standards. Here are those rules again, so that you can have them for easy reference. Pay special attention to those marked with a blue pencil: ✎ .

comma: (,)

after introductory participial phrases: Grabbing the rope, Bo blinked.

after introductory interjections: No, I want no geese present.

after informal salutations: Dear Absalom, you are a rustler.

after long introductory prepositional phrases:
After a very bad giggle, Elenor randomly glanced.

✎ **after multiple introductory prepositional phrases:**
At the back of the boat at the dock, Hiram reflected.

✎ **after introductory dependent clauses (D, I):** As he left, we began again.

after the day and year: On March 12, 2008, Marcus meandered.

after the city and state: Abilene, Texas, was the wrong place to be.

around nonessential (nonrestrictive) clauses:
Daryl Darrel, who is my uncle, decided to demur.

around nonessential participial phrases:
Lou, noticing nothing, nudged the petunia.

✎ **around most appositives:** Mose Osaur, the Nobel Prize winner, replied.

around nouns of direct address: Yes, Luanne, the loam looks lighter.

around parenthetical expressions: Two tons, enough for anyone, arrived.

✎ **before coordinating conjunctions in I,ccI compound sentences:**
Madeline made models, and Hedda had ham.

✎ **between all items in a list:** Eggbert ate eggs, eggs, eggs, eggs, and eggs.

✎ **between *coordinate* adjectives preceding a noun:** Find a short, green stalk.

between contrasts introduced by *not*: I want boats, not goats.

between name and degree or title: Jeffers Thomason, Ph.D.

inside closing quotation marks: "Shut up," he explained.

✎ **NOT between *cumulative* adjectives preceding a noun:** Get five blue ones.

NOT after a short prepositional phrase: For you I found four yew.

NOT between compound subjects/predicates: Sleepy and Dopey were mopey.

NOT between subject and verb: Wrong: July, is named for Julius Caesar.

semicolon: (;)

✎ **between independent clauses if no coordinating conjunction: I;I**
> The time is out of joint; I must depart immediately.

between items in a list if the items themselves contain commas:
> Get me grits; green, growing grass; and grippers.

between independent clauses joined by *however*, etc.:
> I literally laughed; however, you laterally loafed.

colon: (:)

before a list that is not a compound direct object or subject complement:
> Bring this list: apples, paddles, dappled plaids.

before a long formal statement: To my extinguished friends:

✎ **before a long quotation, as in a research paper**

between hours and minutes in time: 6:15

between Bible chapter and verse: John 1:23

after formal salutations: Dear Mr. Applegate:

✎ **between titles and subtitles:** *Walt Whitman: Poet of America*

italics: (*italics*) (In the past, underline was the same thing.)

✎ **title of a book:** *A Tale of Two Cities*

✎ **title of a magazine:** *Life*

title of a work of art: *Mona Lisa*

title of a train or airplane: *Spirit of St. Louis*

✎ **words, letters, and numbers as such:** the word *blubber*, the letter *a*, and the number *5*

foreign language words: *dejà vu*

quotation marks: (" ")

around a direct quotation: Louis XIV said, "I am the state."

commas and periods go inside quotes: "Too late," he explained.

colons and semicolons go outside quotes: Ed said, "Hi"; I fled.

title of short story, poem, song: Please sing "Danny Boy."

✎ **title of article, chapter, or part of publication:**
> The third chapter of *My False Demise* is entitled "Rumors."

NOT to indicate cute, trite, or ungrammatical terms:
> Hi, "Buddies," how about a "pep talk!"

apostrophe: (')

noun made into a possessive: John's quotation

missing letter in a contraction: don't

missing numbers in a year contraction: '47

plurals of letters, numbers, signs, and words as such: *a*'s *5*'s

✎ **with an *s* to show possession after a singular noun:** Dickens's novel

Note that singular nouns ending in *s* still add '*s*: Socrates's philosophy

alone to show possession after a plural noun ending in *s*: `dogs'`
for quotations within quotations:

> `John said, "Hamlet cried, 'Oops!' when he fell."`

✎ **in the contraction of *it* and *is*:** `It's a good day to diet.`
NOT in the possessive pronoun *its*.

✎ **NOT in plural centuries or decades:** `1900s  the 50s`

ellipsis: (. . .)

✎ **to indicate words omitted from quotations**
In Courier the ellipsis is made of five spaces and three periods:

> `There are blank spaces between the periods . . . see?`
> `So it looks like this . . . and not like...this.`

Use three periods if the omission is within a sentence.
Use four periods if the omission occurs right after a sentence ending;
the first is the period at the end of the sentence, followed by the ellipsis:

> `Lincoln could not sleep. . . . Douglass spoke first.`

parenthesis: (( ))

around parenthetical remarks added to a sentence:

> `He said I would be (I wish!) six feet tall.`

brackets: ([ ])

✎ **around words inserted into quoted material:**

> `Johnson notes, "At this time [Dickens] began to weaken."`

When you insert words into quotations, usually for the purpose of clarifying references or enhancing the flow of the sentences, you must enclose your inserted words in brackets like [this] to show that these words were not part of the original quote. Be sure to use true [brackets] rather than (parentheses) or <mathematical symbols>.

dash: (-- or —)

A dash is twice as long as a hyphen. **Hyphen: - Dash: — or --**

✎ **abrupt break in thought:** `So I--wait a minute!--retracted my rebuke.`

✎ **Make a dash in Courier with** `two hyphens, NO spaces--thus.`
In Times Roman you can make a true dash—like this.
NOT to replace proper punctuation.

hyphen: (-)

word divided at end of line
compound written numbers from twenty-one to ninety-nine
fractions used as adjectives: `a three-fourths majority`
prefixes before proper noun or proper adjective: `Pre-Raphaelite`

compound nouns that include prepositional phrases: `father-in-law`
compound adjective when it precedes its noun: a `well-meant lie`
Do NOT use a hyphen (-) **when you intend a dash** (-- or —)
Do NOT hyphenate an adverb to an adjective: a `completely broken door`

question mark: (?)

at the end of an interrogative sentence: `Do you have rhubarb?`
inside closing quotes if part of quote: `He asked, "How about a flower?"`
outside quotes if not part of quote: `Did he say, "I'll allow it louder"?`

period: (.)

at the end of a declarative sentence: `I have three words.`
at the end of a mild imperative sentence: `Please pursue the plot.`
after most abbreviations: `Dr. Trelawney saw the pirates.`
inside closing quotation marks: `He said, "Stop that parrot."`

exclamation point: (!)

after an exclamatory sentence: `The sky is falling!`
after a strong imperative sentence: `Everyone sit up!`
NOT to be cute. Wrong: `Hi! Guess what!!`

GRAMMAR RULES AND ERRORS

Subject / Verb Disagreement s/v

The subject/verb disagreement is the worst error in grammar. The subject of each sentence will be either singular or plural, and the verb must agree with it in number. If the subject is singular, the verb must be singular.

> Wrong: The reason for the numerous objections are obvious.

> Right: The reason for the numerous objections is obvious.

The most common reason for a subject/verb disagreement is the presence of intervening words between the subject and the verb, as in the two examples above. Compound subjects joined by *and* are plural: Bob and Jane are here; compound subjects joined by *or* are singular: Bob or Jane is here. When a gerund phrase is the subject, the verb agrees with the gerund, not the object of the gerund, as in: "*Defeating* the Persians *is* the purpose of the invasion."

Spelling Error sp

With word processors and spell checkers so prevalent, there is no excuse for a spelling error in the final draft of an academic paper. Some spelling errors, however, are surprisingly common, including two shockers: a spelling error in the title of your paper, and the misspelling of your main word, such as spelling *Iliad Illiad* in a paper about *The Iliad*. It never occurs to us that we are misspelling our title or our main word, so we do not think to double-check those.

> Wrong: Shakespear: The Tragic Genius.

> Right: Shakespeare: The Tragic Genius.

Sentence Fragment frag

Advanced academic writing is made of complete sentences. Groups of words that do not make complete thoughts are errors, called *fragments*. One common sentence fragment is to put a period after an introductory dependent clause.

> Wrong: When scientists photographed the squid. They were amazed.

> Right: When scientists photographed the squid, they were amazed.

Another common sentence fragment occurs when you put a period after an introductory participial phrase:

> Wrong: Catching the full force of the gale. Robert crouched.

> Right: Catching the full force of the gale, Robert crouched.

Run-On Sentence R-S

A compound sentence joined by a coordinating conjunction must have a comma before the conjunction, or else it is a run-on sentence.

> Wrong: The sun began to rise and they saw the extent of the damage.

> Right: The sun began to rise, and they saw the extent of the damage.

Comma Splice CS

A comma splice occurs when a comma, rather than a semicolon or comma and coordinating conjunction, is used to connect two independent clauses.

> Wrong: The old man reeled in the fish, the sun began to set.

> Right: The old man reeled in the fish, and the sun began to set.

> Right: The old man reeled in the fish; the sun began to set.

Bad Appositive Construction

An appositive is an interrupting definition. It provides important information immediately, so the reader does not have to read on in confusion. The danger is to forget that appositives must be enclosed in commas—one to start the definition, and one to return to the main idea. If we forget the second comma, we can completely change the meaning of the sentence.

> Wrong: Robert, the mailman is stealing our car.

> Right: Robert, the mailman, is stealing our car.

Notice that in the first sentence there are two men, and we are speaking to Robert. In the second sentence there is one man, and the person being spoken to is not named. The absence of the second appositive comma wreaked all that havoc.

Pronoun Case pron

Subjects and subject complements must use subject pronouns. Direct objects, indirect objects, objects of prepositions, and objects of verbals must use object pronouns. *A subject is a subject, and an object is an object.*

> Wrong: It will be important to you and I.

> Right: It will be important to you and me.

Pronoun Reference *ref*

When multiple nouns precede a pronoun, the antecedent of the pronoun can become unclear. This is called a *reference* error.

> Wrong: James suddenly encountered John, and he looked startled.
>
> Right: James suddenly encountered John, and John looked startled.

Pronoun Number: A *They-Their* Error *ref*

The pronouns *they* and *their* are plural, not singular. When something is *theirs*, then it belongs to a group. Something belonging to an individual is *his* or *hers*.

> Wrong: One of the poets dropped their book.
>
> Right: One of the poets dropped a book.

Misplaced Modifier *mm*

An introductory participial phrase must be set off by a comma and must modify the grammatical subject of the sentence. The modifier is misplaced if the intended target word is present in the sentence, but the modifier modifies the wrong word because of its placement.

> Wrong: Barking furiously at the mailman, Susan shushed Fido.
>
> Right: Barking furiously at the mailman, Fido angered Susan.

Dangling Modifier *DGL or dgl*

A dangling modifier occurs when the intended target word is not even present in the sentence at all.

> Wrong: Barking furiously at the mailman, the day was off to a bad start.
>
> Right: Barking furiously at the mailman, Fido woke us up.

Split Infinitive *We would use the delete mark to remove the inserted word.*

We regard an infinitive as a single word. In advanced academic writing, we do not split the infinitive with an adverb.

> Wrong: Roosevelt began to slowly develop economic programs.
>
> Right: Slowly, Roosevelt began to develop economic programs.

Parallel lists and compounds   //

Lists and compounds need to be constructed with parallel grammar. A list should consist of all adjectives or all nouns, but not a mixture.

> Wrong: Dickens was a novelist, a poet, and spoke often.

> Right: Dickens was a novelist, a poet, and a frequent speaker.

Parallel Tense   t

Tenses should not wander; they should be logical. If you are describing the past, stay in past tense.

> Wrong: Jefferson went home. Soon he is building again.

> Right: Jefferson went home. Soon he was building again.

Double Negative

Many languages, such as Spanish, accept double negatives as a way to intensify an idea, but we do not use double negatives in standard English.

> Wrong: Dickens did *not* know *nothing* about the event.

> Wrong: I am *not* accusing *nobody*.

> Right: Dickens knew nothing about the event.

> Right: I am not accusing anyone.

PROOFREADER'S MARKS

Even correction can be correct. Certain proofreading marks are standard throughout the publishing and academic worlds. You can learn these standard marks now, and see them employed by teachers, professors, and editors in your future.

1.	Delete	I have my very own example.
2.	Insert period	Clouds approached⊙ It rained.
3.	Insert comma	He was strict, stern and serious.
4.	Insert space	Alexander reacted quickly. #
5.	Close up	Suddenly, the bat⌣tle began.
6.	Start new paragraph	It ended. ¶ The next day we departed.
7.	Spell out or spelling error	It was the ④th time that week. ⑤P
8.	Transpose (switch)	It began to suddenly rain ⑪
9.	Awkward wording	It went then higher as a thing gradual. awk
10.	Subject/verb disagreement	The reason for the errors are this. S/V
11.	Insert apostrophe	We saw the brigades slow advance.
12.	Lower case	Dickens was a student of History. lc
13.	Italics	The word chicken sounds funny. ital
14.	Capitalize	The english defeated the armada. cap
15.	Insert hyphen	They fired off a one gun salute. =/
16.	Insert text	It was highest mountain. /the
17.	Leave unchanged	The freezing blue day broke slowly. STET
18.	Sentence fragment	As we began. The door opened. frag
19.	Run-on sentence	Monet painted steadily and the work grew. R-O
20.	Pronoun problem	Everyone lost their sense of humor. pron